Praise for *How to Be a Woman in Technology*

"We live in a day and age when more women in technology really are achieving greater success, rising to senior leadership positions and driving more innovation in their fields. The women who share their stories in these pages fit that mold, and they didn't get there without creativity, resourcefulness, and grit. Their willingness to introspectively share their raw fears, vulnerabilities, challenges, and successes with Cheryl, who communicates those stories so clearly and folds in her own insights, results in a very powerful, inspiring book."

—Dina Moskowitz, CEO, SaaSMAX Corp. (saasmax.com)

"Cheryl makes you feel like you're sitting alongside each of these brilliant women having coffee together. *How to Be a Woman in Technology* reminds you how women have paved the way in this world and motivates you to believe in yourself in a way you never have. In this book, you'll find inspirational vignettes to take with you everywhere, each celebrating a woman who is influencing our future. You'll learn just how much women have done to inform our understanding of all things tech."

—Jaclyn Lindsey, Co-founder and CEO, Kindness.org (kindness.org)

"To Cheryl and the group of women who participated in this project, thank you for the leadership you continue to demonstrate. I'm so very proud of you all! This book is spot on and is a beautiful reminder that, ultimately, it is important to look within and seek what makes you happy."

—Christine Sanni, CEO, ConservGeo (conservgeo.com)

HOW TO BE A
WOMAN
IN TECHNOLOGY
(WHILE FOCUSING ON WHAT MATTERS MOST)

CHERYL O'DONOGHUE, MS

DEDICATION

This book is dedicated to my dear colleague Nosa Eke, owner and publisher of the *Call Center Times*, who passed away unexpectedly on August 16, 2018. Nosa treated all people with great dignity, humanity, and respect. He was one of the good ones. He led by example, and he cared deeply about helping others focus on what matters most.

When I first met Nosa at a contact center event in Chicago more than fifteen years ago, we had an immediate soul connection. Even when my career took me in and out of the contact-center space, Nosa and I kept in touch just to say "hello" and catch up on our families. I'm profoundly saddened by the loss of such a generous and compassionate soul.

Throughout the process of publishing my first book— *How to Be a Woman in Business (while Being True to Yourself)*—Nosa was one of my most vocal champions. His confidence in me and my ability to craft a story humbled me. He believed in the mission of the book, saw its value, and told others about it.

Then, as I was planning this follow-up book, Nosa connected me to Tanya Youvan (vice president, business development, and marketing at Televergence Solutions, Inc.). Tanya, in turn, connected me to Deb Ward (president and CEO at Televergence) who wrote the book foreword and Khali Henderson (senior partner at Buzz Theory Strategies) who connected me to three quarters of the women I interviewed for this book. All of these beautiful souls believe in the great capacity, creativity, and potential of women in technology and are devoted to their growth and advancement for the betterment of all.

To Carretta, Nosa's wife for more than twenty-one years and business partner, and Alyceson-Grace, their daughter who I know will one day blaze great trails in the world of business and beyond, please know that this book was sparked by Nosa's light. My hope is that it will serve to inspire many women, and even a few men, along the way.

In remembrance of Nosa Eke

(1960-2018)

CONTENTS

SECTION I

SECTION II

FOREWORD

By Deborah L. Ward

President and CEO, Televergence Solutions Inc. (televergence.com)

Months before this book was published, I had the opportunity to read Cheryl's manuscript from front to back. What a powerful group of women participated in this book. I believe strongly in the promotion of women in business and technology, and these women share that commitment and desire to pave a path for others to succeed. Their stories will provide support, encouragement, and inspiration to readers at any stage in their career.

I have personally benefitted from having powerful women in my life and want to take a moment to acknowledge five who influenced not only me but so many others in our industry. They are: Nancy Ridge, executive vice president at Telecom Brokers and co-founder of Alliance of Channel Women; Tanya Youvan, vice president of business development at Televergence; Carolyn Bradfield, chief executive officer and chairman of the board at Convey Services; Julia Strow, chief of staff at INCOMPAS; and Angie Kronenburg, chief advocate and general counsel at INCOMPAS. Each of these women has so generously shared her experience, education, values, and knowledge with me. They remind me of the women in this book: women who are quick to offer a helping hand and trusted advice. Their wisdom is available to us in these pages if we are willing to admit that we don't know something and are open to receiving what these women so wholeheartedly offer.

Something else that really resonated with me in this book is the focus on emotional intelligence and the critical role it plays in our careers as women in technology. As we read these women's stories, we get to see their emotional intelligence at work and learn more about ways we too can be more self-aware and can better interact with other people. When we make a conscious effort to become more emotionally intelligent, it forges not only stronger personal relationships but better business relationships as well.

Cheryl's background and knowledge in emotional intelligence leadership is noteworthy. She brings tremendous value to readers on this topic. I found that the information and insights she shares in the second section of this book go far beyond what I have read in several other popular books on the topic. Cheryl is able to take what can be a very confusing and difficult topic and break it down into every day, simplistic terms. She also gives us plenty of takeaways and action items so we can expand our understanding of emotional intelligence and develop it even further.

Developing emotional intelligence can be tough for women in the workplace. Historically, demonstrating an emotional understanding of the world around us has been perceived as a weakness. Yet I know that possessing emotional intelligence is a great strength. And specifically, when you are self-aware—when you can understand yourself and look to yourself, first, in any given situation, to think and process what you can do, do differently, or do even better *before* you turn externally—you can have an incredibly positive impact. The more we can understand and demonstrate our emotional intelligence, the more effective we will all be in our communications and the attainment of our goals, both on a personal and professional level. Additionally, I have found that being emotionally intelligent also means cultivating not just female but male mentors, too, whose perspective is just as needed and valuable to our development.

Another message that was shared by many of the women in this book is the importance for us all to be open to change. We have to be courageous and not be paralyzed by the fear of doing something different or new, especially if we are in an unhappy or unfulfilling situation. Personally, I was born and raised in California, and I started my business there as well. But I always felt like a fish out of water because I was a cowgirl at heart. One day, I decided to make a change because the fear of the unknown was less painful than living an inauthentic life. I sold nearly everything and moved myself, family, and business to Nashville…and I never looked back. For one of the first times, I was aligned fully with my core beliefs and values, and that led to a series of amazing transformations. My hope is that through the stories in this book, readers will see their own possibilities for positive, transformational change and will have the courage to turn those possibilities into realities.

Finally, I also hope that this book reminds all women in technology to get involved in moving our industry forward, and our place in it, no matter what our job title is. This is yet another message that came through quite clearly. For me, since I was one of the very few women CEOs and/or owners in the telecommunications industry, I found that it was important to be visible to other women and to work on their behalf. This has led me to serve as the first chairwoman of INCOMPAS (formerly known as Comptel), a role I've held for nearly five years, and to continue my active involvement in national organizations such as the National Association of Women Business Owners (NAWBO), the Alliance of Channel Women (ACW), and the Channel Partners' Women in the Channel (WIC) Mentor Program, as well as numerous local organizations, including the Women in Technology of Tennessee. In recent years I've been motivated to do even more. In 2017, my company, Televergence, became certified as a Women's Business Enterprise (WBE) though the Women's Business Enterprise National Council (WBENC). WBENC's mission is to fuel economic growth globally by identifying, certifying, and facilitating the development of women-owned businesses—a mission I share that continues to be dear to me over the course of my decades-long career.

As women in technology, we may still have a way to go, but look at how much progress we've made. Let's use this book as a launching pad for our next great adventure. And, as the title suggests, let's consider using this book to cultivate our own unique brand of women who work in technology—women who are focused on what matters most.

SECTION

I

CHAPTER 1 _____
Our Conversation Starts Here
_____

Consider this.

As you're reading this book, there are more than 7.6 billion people on this whirling, beautiful planet called Earth. Yep, that sure is a lot of people. And of all those 7.6 billion people, I have the unbelievably good fortune to have you, yes you, holding this book and reading these words. You and I, in this very moment, are having a real connection. How exceptional is that?

The other thing I find exceptional about our connection is that I know you have been attracted to this book in particular for a specific reason (or reasons) not-yet-but soon-to-be revealed to you as you read the fascinating stories and insights women share throughout these pages.

I know that through our connection, something in this book will prompt a thought or an action that just might change your life in an unusually positive and meaningful way. I know that through our connection, you will see real-life experiences of other women that just might resonate with you in a way that will alter your perspective and outlook on what it means to be a woman in technology.

And this is exactly what I love most about books. Books are personal. Whatever is in that book becomes a part of you. You invest time in reading the book, and in return, you get something for that investment. Perspective. Insights. Actionable tips. And more.

So, let me lay out for you the tone and intention of this book and some thoughts on how you can get the most from it.

The tone of this book is conversational—and a bit unconventional. I didn't follow the generally accepted guidelines for writing a typical nonfiction business book. What I followed was my gut and a picture I had in my mind of you and me sitting down, enjoying a few of our favorite beverages, and having a series of conversations.

As far as the intention of this book, it's simply to give back by paying it forward. Every person you'll meet as you read each chapter truly cares about your journey and about the industry from which they earn a paycheck—technology. They were all excited to participate in this project not because they are being compensated (they are not), but because the reward for them is to share their feedback and experiences in the hope that at least one reader will find it to be of use.

To be of use. To have a useful purpose. That is my driver as well and why I am writing this book and the one that preceded it—*How to Be a Woman in Business (While Being True to Yourself)*. My desire is to be of use to you by bringing you stories from real women who are unafraid to speak their truths and to share with you their journeys to discovering what matters most to them in their careers and lives. At the beginning of each chapter, I will share with you my own stories and thoughts as a longtime businesswoman, manager, business coach, and human potential educator. The first part of the book offers stories you can read sequentially or out of order. It doesn't really matter. Read them in whatever sequence makes sense to you.

Then in the second part of the book, I will share with you some of my work in the field of Emotional Intelligence and why I believe your knowledge and application of a few Emotional Intelligence-boosting practices can help you get the most enjoyment out of your career and your life. Emotional intelligence (EI) is the capacity to recognize your own, and other people's emotions; to know the differences between emotions and label them appropriately; and to use emotional information to guide thinking and behavior.

I will also share an exercise to help you focus on what emotional needs matter most to you at this time. This is where many of us get stuck in our lives. We focus on *soooo* much, but not necessarily on the one or two things that actually mean something to us or have the most merit or value. When this happens, as it often does, we feel out of sync.

To understand what matters most, we need to rise up and take control of our lives and the direction in which we're heading. For some of us, that will mean breaking out of molds that no longer work for us. For others it will mean getting out of our comfort zones or stepping out of the shadows and into the spotlight.

When you can put your finger on what matters most to you and take purposeful, emotionally intelligent action, your professional and personal life will evolve in a way that will bring you immense satisfaction and relief.

And isn't that what we need more of in our chaotic world of seemingly infinite options and opportunities? A bit of order. A bit of peace. A way of being that feels good and makes the best sense for you at this time. I'm biased, I'll admit it, but I think you'll be able to get some pretty darn good use out of this second section as well.

Ready? Let's get to it.

CHAPTER 2 ⸻

A Conversation with Khali Henderson

Senior Partner at BuzzTheory Strategies (buzztheorystrategies.com)

⸻

> The smarter the journalists are, the better off society
> is. [For] to a degree, people read the press to inform
> themselves—and the better the teacher, the better the
> student body.
> — Warren Buffett, American business magnate, investor,
> and philanthropist

> The way to achieve your own success is to be willing to
> help somebody else get it first.
> — Iyanla Vanzant, speaker

First, a Few of My Thoughts

I can't wait for you to read what Khali Henderson has to say in this chapter. She has been a successful journalist and editor-in-chief at prominent technology industry publications for more than twenty years. She is one of the top tech journalists in the US (and I would venture to say, the world, though she is too humble to put that forth, so I will). This unusual vantage point gives us all a glimpse of where we've been, which is important to remember because it has the power to provide distinct insights into where we may be heading.

But that's not all. While Khali is a longtime observer of the tech industry, she also has an inside view into what it's like to be a woman *in* tech, because she has held positions consulting to tech companies. In her current position as senior partner with BuzzTheory Strategies, a firm that helps companies across the technology value chain create and monetize business relationships, she serves as the company's marketing and media specialist and tech channel expert. This dual perspective over the course of her career as a tech spectator and insider brings extra insights, and we get to be the beneficiaries of her wisdom. Lucky, lucky us.

Yet what makes me one of Khali's biggest fans is this: she is *our* biggest fan. I included the quote from Iyanla Vanzant at the beginning of this chapter because I believe Khali embodies the sentiment completely—her own definitions of success are built upon the idea of lifting others up. If you have not experienced the benefits of following Vanzant's advice firsthand, I encourage you to put it into action immediately. Help somebody else be successful. You will be astounded by your experience. I had to learn this lesson the hard way.

When I started my career a few decades ago, I operated from a position of scarcity. The jobs I was most interested in were being given to men. Over time, companies began to consider women for some of these roles, but those instances were few and far between—and usually only one woman sat at the leadership table. I was coached by my male mentors at the time to compete aggressively for those roles. To treat other women (and men) as adversaries in my pursuit of the golden ring. I had always been a good student, so I quickly internalized what they had to say and took action. I excelled in the art of business strategy and positioning—the art of war. I received coveted promotions, titles, and pay raises. I was at the leadership table, but there was a substantive cost: I felt like garbage. Forgive me for not offering a more eloquent description; it was that bad. Something had to give. Through my misery, I gained insight and vowed to never be untrue to myself again.

My truth is that I'm a natural cheerleader of other humans; I genuinely want the best for all. I am a maximizer, not a competitor. I am a human developer, not a destroyer. I believe there is no shortage of opportunities when you are playing to your strengths in an emotionally intelligent way.

After I reconnected to my truth, I went on to create a satisfying career as an operations, communications, and organizational development leader across three vertical markets—financial services, corporate education, and healthcare. I am forever grateful for those early experiences, which resulted in me becoming a colleague and leader with whom others would like to work. And being this type of businesswoman felt infinitely better than garbage!

I encourage you to get to know your truth and then be of use to others. And like Khali, look for opportunities to give others—especially women—a chance to shine, develop their strengths, and get their unique messages out into the world. Look for opportunities to give others a chance to be successful according to their own personal definitions of success, which, by the way, may be very different from your own version. I do believe this is one of the surest ways to abundance. When you amplify others' success, you'll attract people and opportunities that will lead to a feeling of fulfillment and deep satisfaction. This, in my modest opinion, is one of the highest vibrations of success. You know what to do. There really is enough of the good stuff for us all.

Speaking of the good stuff, here are some seriously terrific thoughts from Khali.

"It was 1988 when I started my journalism career, and when people would ask me what I did for a living and I told them I was a writer in the tech space, they would glaze over," remembers Khali. "They felt sorry for me, thinking I drew the short straw in landing the worst possible career."

Khali, on the other hand, could think of nothing more exciting. While journalists for other industries covered the same round of stories each year, Khali covered brand-new stories daily. There was never a shortage of new information, new technologies, and new companies on which to report. For her, being a technology journalist was the opportunity of a lifetime.

> **You can work for any company and be in the tech department. So, if you really like sports, you can work in tech at a sporting company. If you're interested in fashion, the fashion industry has a tremendous need for tech professionals."**

Khali has had a front row seat to countless technological advancements that have forever altered our human experience, and she has had the added perspective of being on the inside, as an internal consultant and team member at tech and tech-focused companies. From this vantage point, she has come to see that we all can benefit when we expand our definition and vision of tech careers, recognizing that women may limit their opportunities by thinking a career in tech is reserved only for those who work for well-known tech firms. "You don't have to work at a company like Cisco or Oracle to be in tech," she says. "You can work for any company and be in the tech department. So, if you really like sports, you can work in tech at a sporting company. If you're interested in fashion, the fashion industry has a tremendous need for tech professionals."

For women to continue to make advancements in technology, they must own the contributions they make in the technology channel. In Khali's experience, she has found it not uncommon for women, including herself at one time, to suffer from "imposter syndrome." In this respect, women in tech can feel like imposters or pretenders because they hold a false belief that only those working at tech companies and in roles associated with programming and software development have the "real" tech jobs. Sadly, this narrow thinking is further inculcated in cultures at those companies that identify tech employees as staff members who create the technology and categorize other employees as non-tech staff. By doing so, these companies unknowingly discount the education, training, and expertise of millions of other workers who are, in fact, holding positions in tech, including those who sell, market, and support tech solutions.

Khali's journalism coverage of the tech industry over the years also gave her a unique perspective of the evolution and fusing of technology with traditional business functions, from finance and operations to sales and marketing. All functions come with a need to be technologically astute. "I'm now working at a company in the functional area of MarTech—marketing technology," she notes. "You cannot be an effective marketer today without also being a technologist. The need for marketing technologists will only grow. These are attractive jobs where creativity and innovation are encouraged." The same logic applies to other functional areas.

> **It takes great effort to stay abreast of emerging technologies, and there are few experts available to teach others. Numerous women, in particular, have a great desire to get up to speed, so they form their own groups to fill in any knowledge gaps."**

Khali sees that women have a great capacity to shift company cultures because many women have leadership styles that tend to be more collaborative and less competitive. Women also have a deep interest in assisting others and their companies through knowledge acquisition. "It takes great effort to stay abreast of emerging technologies, and there are few experts available to teach others," says Khali. "Numerous women, in particular, have a great desire to get up to speed, so they form their own groups to fill in any knowledge gaps."

A great example is Cloud Girls (cloudgirls.org)—an open, vendor-neutral, not-for-profit community of female thought leaders and technology advocates dedicated to educating themselves and their stakeholders (the organizations and customers they serve) about the vast and dynamic cloud ecosystem. By exploring emerging market and technical trends, advocating best practices, and building community consensus, Cloud Girls is fostering the next wave of women in technology. In 2011, Khali was invited to this group through her network of women in tech, and she now serves on their board. She is also a past board member for Alliance of Channel Women (allianceofchannelwomen.org) and Technology Channel Association.

Cloud Girls members participate in virtual meetings where a team of four or five Cloud Girls researches an emerging topic and shares what they've learned with the group. It's like a force multiplier, in that you get the benefit of their work without having to do it yourself. At a recent meeting, the members discussed distributed ledger (blockchain) technology and its implications for businesses and clients.

 Many of the women just starting their tech careers don't realize that women were the pioneers of computing, making considerable and important early discoveries. They think that women being in tech is a more current trend, but it isn't. It's just that somewhere along our timeline we forgot that we played a significant role in launching this industry."

"We're not sitting still," Khali emphasizes. "Cloud Girls realized they had an opportunity to help educate women on new cloud technologies and help them become practice leaders inside their own organizations. These ladies are very eager to learn and willing to spend extra time outside their jobs to train and share knowledge with others. And a significant number of them are taking their careers into their own hands by lobbying to be their company's internal cloud experts. They are not waiting for someone from the top to hand them the title or for one of their male colleagues to be given the opportunity. They are taking the initiative, doing the work, and providing cloud leadership for their companies and clients. They feel it's their responsibility to break new ground and make that happen."

Women are no strangers to leading the way for others and doing groundbreaking work in tech. While movies such as *Hidden Figures* help to provide a historical perspective of women in the early days of computing technology, Khali has found that young women, especially, benefit from remembering what other women have accomplished before them. "Many of the women just starting their tech careers don't realize that women were the pioneers of computing, making considerable and important early discoveries. They think that women being in tech is a more current trend, but it isn't. It's just that somewhere along our timeline we forgot that we played a significant role in launching this industry. When computing started to boom and become more lucrative, the men who were running the companies realized they wanted to be doing the type of work women in tech were advancing. They took over the positions held by these women technology pioneers and hired other men to fill new roles."

Khali also suggests that younger women should recognize and value the work of women who have been battling inequality in the tech industry for decades, and she encourages them to take a leading role in protecting the gains made by these women. "I would like nothing more for young women today to continue to benefit from the work of those women who had come before them, to work in a culture that treats all employees equally," she says. "It should be a given, but that often is not the case. If we don't encourage a culture of equality, cultivate it, and value it, our gains can go away just as they did in the early days of computing."

“ Participate in mentoring programs or any other program that the organization has in place for you to get to know senior managers and understand your company culture.”

Khali has found that sometimes younger women get turned off by their female predecessors who openly voiced displeasure at what they found to be unfair discriminatory business practices. They describe these women as "feminists" or what some refer to as "feminazis." "I don't think we need to be pushing our past struggles and accomplishments down our younger colleagues' throats," reminds Khali. "But we need to figure out a way for them to have that understanding of what was sacrificed to get to this point and pass along to them the desire to protect and defend our progress and participate in its growth going forward."

One way to continue to cultivate a culture that is more balanced for all and in better alignment with workers' values is for women to get to know the leaders at their organizations—male and female. "Participate in mentoring programs or any other program that the organization has in place for you to get to know senior managers and understand your company culture," advises Khali. "Also, if you are a woman who gains any kind of authority, you must use it to the best of your ability to create the types of policies that foster gender equality or neutrality."

Khali is quick to point out that any work done to support women must not be done in a way that excludes. She believes the goal is not to be against men, but the goal is to be for all people. She recommends that women cultivate men in their organizations to be their allies and peers because there are amazing men who want equality for all, and their numbers are growing. One of the positive effects of the myriad women-focused movements of today is that more men in the workplace have a growing awareness of what their mothers, daughters, wives, friends, and colleagues have experienced. They are more tuned in and willing to take actions to remediate or eliminate harassment, bias, and inequality.

As a vocal advocate for women in tech for the better part of her career, Khali leaves us with a parting thought and a direct request to take an active role in promoting gender equality for our own children starting at an early age. She cautions, "We really have a serious situation in our society where we very quickly indoctrinate young children that gender is not gender equal."

Khali referred to a study that was reported widely a few years ago that researched a statistically significant sample size of children who were entering kindergarten and then followed up with them at the end of kindergarten as they were promoted to first grade. Right before the students entered kindergarten, the researchers shared with them a story about a smart child who was able to do amazing things in life. They then asked each of the girls, individually, if they could imagine the story being about them, and the girls said "yes" they could imagine the story being about them. They did the same activity with each of the boys. All the boys said they could imagine the story being about them. Fast-forward to the end of kindergarten. Researchers shared the same story, in the same manner, and with the same group of children, asking each of them the same question: could they imagine the story being about them? The boys' answers did not change, but the girls' answers did. A notable number of those same girls said "no," they could not imagine that the story was about them. They told the researchers "the story is about a boy."

" If in kindergarten our girls have begun to go from 'I can' to 'I can't,' imagine what an issue this becomes when those same girls get to high school or college and they've had twelve to fourteen years of this programming."

"Our socialization process elevates boys over girls," says Khali. "It asks the question 'what is happening in that pivotal year that a young girl goes from thinking she has unlimited potential, to being a second-class citizen?'"

While it may be easy to point fingers at the education system, Khali doesn't think that's entirely fair. "I think the responsibility starts at home, no matter the gender of your child. Children pick up gender cues all around them—school, the internet, TV, friends, grandparents, parents, you name it. I think women, specifically, are in a very good position to be more deliberate about teaching our children the value system we want them to adopt and internalize. And we must start right away. If in kindergarten our girls have begun to go from 'I can' to 'I can't,' imagine what an issue this becomes when those same girls get to high school or college and they've had twelve to fourteen years of this programming."

To start, Khali suggests that mothers of girls *and* boys ensure they are not unknowingly fostering any gender-biased beliefs, such as the ideas that girls are not good in math and science or boys are less verbal than girls. Both these beliefs are generalizations that are not true for all.

"My husband and I raised boys, and even though they had me, a working mother, as a role model, I should have done more to help them understand how girls are treated differently from boys in society," she reflects. "I didn't think to have those types of conversations with my sons as they were growing up. But we're having them now."

"My sons are very respectful of women, yet they struggle as young men because they are painted as the enemy, being portrayed as sexually aggressive and discriminatory just because they are male. It upsets them. I tell them that even though they may not be acting this way with women personally, their peers are, and they need to be aware of it. I think if I had more conversations with them as they were growing up and gave them specific examples of how girls are treated differently and at different ages, that would have had a positive impact—on them and the girls they came in contact with."

❝ For girls to make strides in tech—and in life— we need to help all children use their voices and construct their messages so they can have open and meaningful in-person conversations with others."

"We also have to help our children connect with others on a human basis," she adds. "One of the unintended consequences of technology is that people aren't developing deeper relationships with other people. Our child might have over five hundred Facebook friends, but she or he is lucky to have one or two close friends. And children struggle not only with creating friendships with their followers but communicating with others they don't know. For girls to make strides in tech—and in life—we need to help all children use their voices and construct their messages so they can have open and meaningful in-person conversations with others. As our world gets more complex, this will continue to grow as a needed and valued skill."

More about Khali Henderson

Khali Henderson is senior partner for BuzzTheory Strategies (buzztheorystrategies.com). She has more than twenty-five years of marketing, communications, and content development experience in the technology space. Perhaps best known for her leadership at Channel Partners, the telecom and IT industry's leading channel media and events brand, Khali is one of the country's foremost experts on channel strategy and marketing.

Khali has also developed and managed marketing and public relations programs for a range of technology companies and trade associations. At BuzzTheory, she heads up business development and serves as the chief content officer.

Khali has recently served on the boards of the Telecom Channel Association, Cloud Girls (cloudgirls.org), and Alliance of Channel Women (allianceofchannelwomen.org). An avid fan of science as well as science fiction, Khali is as likely to be found at a Comicon or Star Trek event as she is at a cutting-edge technology symposium. Her favorite pastimes are reading and hanging out with her husband, four sons, their dog Willy, and their cat Tribble.

Follow Khali on LinkedIn (Khali Henderson) and Twitter (khalihenderson). She can also be contacted at khenderson@buzztheorystrategies.com.

CHAPTER 3 _____

A Conversation with Jean O'Neill

Vice President Channel at Cyxtera Technologies (cyxtera.com)

_____

We need to accept that we won't always make the right
decisions, that we'll screw up royally sometimes—
understanding that failure is not the opposite of success,
it's part of success.
—Arianna Huffington, author, columnist, businesswoman

There are three classes of people: those who see,
those who see when they are shown,
and those who do not see.
—Leonardo da Vinci, painter, sculptor, architect, inventor

First, a Few of My Thoughts

How do you know when it's time for a change? And how do you
take that leap forward when you know the time has come? Every
woman needs to be able to answer these questions for herself.
These are life's mission-critical questions, right up there with the
biggies such as "Why am I here?" and "Where am I going?"

I know it is time for a change when my emotional pain around
a job or a relationship (sometimes both) becomes so acute that it
exceeds my fear of the unknown. Whenever I find myself feeling
this way, I know I need to take action. And now, with some years
under my belt, I can say that the leaps from my launching pad of
pain turned out to be exactly what I needed at the time, allowing
me to grow in wondrous ways I would never have imagined.

One example that comes to mind was when I was working for an international training and consulting firm, and we had just merged into a group of three similar companies. At the time I was working as a senior vice president in charge of marketing. Over the course of a few months, I took on the added role of running training content development and delivery operations for not only my firm, but for the other three groups that formed the new corporation. Overnight, my job expanded fourfold. I was tasked with learning each company's business operation and subsequently combining operations where it made sense. In the process of taking on these other responsibilities, I became the hatchet lady who had the unpleasant task of letting go exceptionally talented individuals because their roles were duplicated in the newly formed organization.

Remember the movie *Up in the Air* with George Clooney and Anna Kendrick? Ryan Bingham (Clooney) works for a human resources consultancy firm specializing in job-termination assistance. At one point, Ryan's boss assigns him to bring Natalie (Kendrick) on his next round of layoffs to show her the termination ropes. The reactions of those they fired stuck with me. I've seen those faces many times throughout my career. *Up in the Air* is a pitch-perfect depiction of what my average workday had become.

Rather than creating new business, a strength I possess, I was embroiled in deconstructing businesses to the point where there was little left to reorganize and grow. And it was hard for me to *not* care about the people who lost their jobs, no matter what I did to help ease their transition and attract new employment opportunities. That was my point of pain. The point where I took the jump, knowing that the parachute would open for me. I gracefully exited the organization to start my own consulting practice, and because I negotiated an exit package, I managed to make the transition without any loss of income. The change also enabled me to be more available at home, spending precious time with my husband and two-year-old daughter. I remember the sweet feeling of relief when I took the leap. Deep, deep relief so palpable I can still feel it today.

Did I have a plan before I took the leap? I had an *idea* of a plan, but all I needed was to map out one action step at a time, one day at a time, and then keep working that plan. Thinking too far in advance just brought me more confusion and dampened my resolve. One of my favorite quotes is from Peter Drucker, who said, "When you're looking for a way, any map will do." I took those words to heart and didn't agonize over the details. It's a guiding principle I have turned to time and time again. It's my answer to the question "How do I make this happen?" and the fuel for nearly all of my personal and professional accomplishments.

So how does it work for you? How do you know when it's time to make a change, and how do you make that change happen? Take some time to think about this and consider what other women have done to answer these questions for themselves. We really do have *so* much in common, and our collective experiences have a tremendous capacity to lift us up and show us the way.

This chapter with Jean O'Neill is filled with exceedingly relatable and inspiring stories and perspectives. She is a compelling speaker and advocate for women who work in technology. She speaks from the heart—and speaks her mind.

She encourages all of us to pay attention to our personal brand, build meaningful business relationships, and above all, listen to the gentle nudges of our own intuition telling us to take a leap of faith when it's aligned with what's most important to us.

"A funny thing happens to me whenever I travel, even overseas," muses Jean. "Someone will inevitably ask me for directions, and, coincidentally, I usually have them!"

Jean will tell you it's because she's a 5'10" blonde who just stands out. After talking with her for only a moment, though, you get the sense that's not quite the whole story. This is a woman who exudes confidence from her first hello. Take a look at the recommendations on her LinkedIn profile, and you'll see that she backs her presence with plenty of substance. She is someone who helps her business partners "navigate the complexities of dynamic, complex organizations with ease" and her preparedness is "second to none."

What can we learn from Jean? Plenty.

For example, Jean believes that many women get sidetracked by failure early in their careers. Not because they fail, per se, but because of the guilt associated with it. "Failure absolutely is an option, and a good one at that," she notes. "You need to learn to fail and learn to fail gracefully. Failure is not an absolute though."

Jean cautions women who are too hard on themselves after experiencing a setback. "Guilt was a big part of my upbringing. I gave it up when I gave up being Catholic. I had to learn that guilt only serves a purpose in small amounts. It can help prevent you from making the same mistake twice, yes, but in most cases, you have nothing to feel guilty about when you fail."

Admittedly, Jean struggled with allowing herself to fail when she was younger. "I gave myself more latitude to fail only when my professional career trajectory rose," she says. "Yet the converse really is true. When you're younger, that's the time to fail because you're new in the workforce and early in your career."

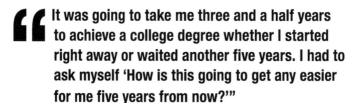 **It was going to take me three and a half years to achieve a college degree whether I started right away or waited another five years. I had to ask myself 'How is this going to get any easier for me five years from now?'"**

Another pearl of insight Jean learned along the way was to be open to possibilities, even when your past may suggest otherwise. In her late twenties, she found herself at a crossroad. She was divorced (she married at age eighteen), co-parenting her son without financial support, and working in retail management. Her husband had not allowed her to pursue a college education.

"Once I was out on my own, I kept saying there is no way I can afford to go to college, to juggle that with raising a child and working a full-time job that barely covered my bills," remembers Jean. "But I was able to look at the broader possibility. It was going to take me three and a half years to achieve a college degree whether I started right away or waited another five years. I had to ask myself 'How is this going to get any easier for me five years from now?'"

She took a leap of faith and began earning her degree in communications. Shortly thereafter, she was presented with yet another opportunity to be open to possibilities rather than be hamstrung by her past.

Jean relates, "I had been working for ten years in retail management at a high-end fashion store. There was a Georgia Tech student who worked there part-time who I got to know. One day he mentioned that he had a friend who owned a software company who was looking for someone to do marketing. He suggested I talk to him."

❝❝ I didn't know that I couldn't do a particular job. The way I looked at it, I never tried it, so obviously I never failed at it."

She got the job and began her career in technology right when email and the internet began to be used in the workplace. The communicator in her saw the power of the internet immediately. She was hooked. Her job working at the software company led to another position at a technical recruiting firm at the time the internet exploded. "It was amazing!" says Jean "I was working with graphic designers, content people, coders, engineers, everybody who was literally building the web. While I wasn't an engineer, my passion for and contribution to tech was (and continues to be) more macro than micro. I can see how all the pieces fit together to be used to improve our world."

As her career advanced, Jean found that one of her success factors was that she just jumped into new roles without worry. "I was too dumb to know any better!" she jokes. "I didn't know that I couldn't do a particular job. The way I looked at it, I never tried it, so obviously I never failed at it."

Jean's attitude freed her to achieve. To illustrate this point, she relates an experience she had selling online marketing for a client of hers—Showtime. "I had to find companies that would fund Showtime by sponsoring ads and events to drive traffic to Showtime's web-based media sites. I was the person who didn't know that you didn't just pick up the phone to cold call Microsoft and say, 'hey I want to showcase your tool, and I want you to give it to me for free.'"

One thing in particular that Jean takes seriously is self-discovery. She believes you must invest in building a personal brand based on a deep knowledge of yourself. She also notes that on the path to self-discovery, you will have to sidestep some potholes.

"When I first started in tech, I had a woman as a manager, whom I respected, who successfully founded and operated her own company," remembers Jean. "Her biggest criticism of me was she thought I needed to be more passive and accommodating, like her, to succeed. She called it being 'soft.' When I heard that advice, I was so conflicted. That might have worked for her while she was running her company, which was based in the south, but the intellectual in me didn't buy it."

> ❝❝ **Find the things you do well, and do more of those things. When you have something you don't do well, you team up with those who do."**

In the years that followed, Jean would receive reviews from other managers who would tell her how wonderful her performance was and then provide her a list of five "weaknesses" on which to work. Although this was a typical management practice at the time, it just didn't resonate with her. She strongly believed her success was dependent on finding out what she did well and developing those strengths further, rather than spending time improving on weaknesses or lesser talents. Right around this time, the book *Now Discover Your Strengths* came out by Marcus Buckingham and Donald O. Clifton. The book was a revelation for Jean.

"That book just made so much sense to me," Jean exclaims. "Find the things you do well, and do more of those things. When you have something you don't do well, you team up with those who do. Why would I dilute my strengths by wasting time on the things I didn't do as well?"

Jean was on a speaker's panel recently for a women's technology group. One of the women in the audience asked the panel for guidance on an issue she was facing, which reminded Jean of her own earlier experiences in understanding how strengths work. The woman explained that she was the person on the team who, when new hires came on board, showed them the ropes, sharing information on how work gets done. Her colleagues, who were primarily men, had suggested that her behavior with new hires made her appear too weak. She asked the panel about ways she could change herself to conform with how she thought the men wanted her to behave.

❝❝ When you are contorting yourself to accommodate, the fit is wrong."

"I got heated," Jean admits. "First of all, I told this woman that I would hire her on the spot because she is *exactly* the type of person I want on my team. I told her she is not the problem. The problem is that she's at the wrong place or in the wrong job, or both. When you are contorting yourself to accommodate, the fit is wrong."

Jean also believes that women, especially in a male-dominated industry such as technology, are prone to devalue their strengths and the assets they possess. She shared an example of a recent experiment in which researchers gave a fake job description to ten women and ten men who had the same professional credentials and comparable work experience. The job description was for a position in a tech firm that was above the pay-grade for all twenty of the experiment participants. When the researchers asked each of the individuals if they felt they were qualified for the position, nine of the ten women said "no" and ten of the ten men said "yes."

> **In my opinion, we need to be okay with NOT having it all. As does the world around us. Having it all, and all it implies, is a confusing, damaging message for women that can take years to unravel."**

"When you're in technology, you can't help but notice inequalities," says Jean. "We have to do our part to know and value our strengths. That's a great place to start. And be wary of messages you get from others, including media-driven messages about what you should or should not do."

While Jean admits that the recent media attention on women's issues can serve as a powerful catalyst for change, she also cautions us to pay attention when a message doesn't line up with our values. "Do you notice that men are never told they can 'have it all'?" asks Jean. "They are encouraged to focus on their careers, because it's nearly impossible to have it all. But women are regularly fed this message that we can have it all if we just try hard enough—work all day, take care of the kids, go to your child's school event, bake cookies for the bake sale, volunteer at church, clean the house, focus on your partner's needs, and then take care of your own needs. In my opinion, we need to be *okay* with NOT having it all. As does the world around us. Having it all, and all it implies, is a confusing, damaging message for women that can take years to unravel."

"You need to stand up and show your truth. You need to show the world your strengths and that you are smart enough to acknowledge what isn't your strength by finding somebody else to fill a need, be that a nanny, a cook, a family member, a spouse, a tutor, a dog walker, whoever."

And sometimes you have to stand up and show your true self to the people who can be your harshest critics—your family. To explain, Jean shares a story of when she was riding high in her professional and personal life while based in Atlanta. Her mother had a serious health set back, and Jean, being the only daughter in a family of eight, made the decision to do what her conservative family expected of her. She was adaptable and moved back to Texas to assist her mother.

Jean wonders, "Why is it that you can be seen by most the people you know as being a high-functioning, fruitful adult, yet when you're around your parents and siblings you're back to being viewed as a kid again, which in my case was the youngest of six with five older and larger brothers, ranging from 6'2" to 6'8". And I was never the coddled little sister! I fought my own fights."

Jean will tell you she comes from a long line of pessimistic people. Her family dinners, still to this day, are filled with quick wit, sharp tongues, and plenty of personally directed digs. Fortunately, Jean saw her return home as an opportunity to put her growth and development over the years to good use.

"I decided to conduct my own social experiment on myself," she shares. "It was quite a shock to be back home in what I can only describe as a quasi-toxic environment of oppression and pessimism with people who believed that anything that could go wrong will, and, if it goes right, it will still go wrong eventually. For two weeks I made a conscious decision to find the positive in everything I experienced being back at home."

At the end of the two weeks, Jean had made a huge paradigm shift which she took to like a fish to water. Her world changed in remarkable ways just by being positive and grateful. She began to attract new people and exciting opportunities. "That shift affected me deep down to my core. Part of me wonders how my life would have been different had I experienced the shift earlier, but the other part knows that things happen when you're ready for them to happen."

Jean also knows that self-discovery and personal development is an ongoing process, and even when you've made meaningful progress, you will be tested. That brings us to Leonardo da Vinci's quote at the beginning of this chapter: "There are three classes of people: those who see, those who see when they are shown, and those who do not see." Usually tests come when interacting with "people who do not see" or, said another way, people with views and values different from your own. Just as Jean had her fair share of tests when she moved back to Texas, she raised a lot of eyebrows when she decided to leave Texas and take a hiatus from work.

"I had been working since I was nine years old," Jean shares. "I started with my brothers cleaning toilets and emptying trash at my father's office complex. Numerous jobs and forty plus years later, I found myself hitting the wall. It was scary to let go. Being single and raising a child without financial support, I learned a long time ago to be frugal. I saved up money but was saving it for a rainy day. Yet the positive person in me said 'Why not spend it on a sunny day?'"

That's exactly what Jean did. Bolstered by an incredibly supportive person (whom she later married), within weeks, she quit her job and moved—this time to San Diego. A year and a half later, while she knew San Diego was the place for her, she also knew it was time to immerse herself in her career again.

As Jean started working her large network of contacts, an odd pattern emerged. The men she contacted consistently responded that they knew she was capable but had to pass because she hadn't worked in more than a year, even though she continued to provide consulting while on hiatus. On the other hand, the women with whom she connected never mentioned the gap, and ultimately it was a woman who played an instrumental role in her landing her next job.

The job search tested her in other ways as well. She received job offers for half the salary she knew she was worth. Other offers had good money attached to them, but she wouldn't be using her talents, or the jobs involved work that was below her capabilities. She knew what a good job fit felt like, so she kept working her network.

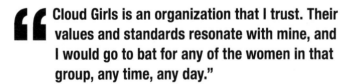 **Cloud Girls is an organization that I trust. Their values and standards resonate with mine, and I would go to bat for any of the women in that group, any time, any day."**

Then one day she interviewed for a vice present of channel position for a data center company. She had never held a position with that title, nor had she done the job before, but she knew she could do it. She also knew the company was the right one for her. After she interviewed with the top two C-level executives, who happened to be men, she reached out to a female in her networking group who knew them both. The woman sent the men a text that read, "I'm on the phone with Jean O'Neill, and if you don't hire her, you're both idiots!" They responded back that she'd just moved to the top of the list. Jean landed the job.

Jean is adamant that women currently working in or planning to work for technology companies must get involved with tech-focused networking and support groups. "This wonderful woman did not have a personal relationship with me. She knew of me. She was in Cloud Girls with me, and we ran in the same circles. Cloud Girls is an organization that I trust. Their values and standards resonate with mine, and I would go to bat for any of the women in that group, any time, any day."

As a parting thought, Jean wants to encourage women working in technology to do all they can to support women entrepreneurs in tech, especially those seeking funding. It's one of the reasons she serves on the board of SaaSMAX Corporation and actively promotes the work of their founder Dina Moskowitz, as well as another woman entrepreneur, Ana Bermudez, who created TAGit, the mobile app that TV viewers use to buy items from their favorite TV shows.

The disparity in funding women in technology is alarming, and Jean believes that many men are shutting women out only because they are female and not because anything is lacking in their business plan. "You could write a whole book on this topic," Jean notes.

Interestingly, a few weeks after I interviewed Jean, a new book came out by author Emily Chang, featuring the many inequalities of women working in technology. The book is called *Brotopia: Breaking Up the Boys' Club of Silicon Valley*. The numbers speak for themselves. According to Chang's research, women-led companies get only two percent of venture capital funding, and the number of women who get pushed out of their jobs when their salaries start to rise is staggering. This book is a must-read.

"Most people think of technology as being an advanced field—just look at all the nationalities we embrace—and yet, it's far from advanced in this respect," observes Jean. "Women like Dina Moskowitz and Ana Bermudez who are committed to advancing opportunities for other women, inspire me. Women who are successful in spite of an everyday battle to follow their path, inspire me. Women in technology inspire me. It's a daunting task, but we have to put ourselves out there. We have to go out on a limb. It's time for us all to be heroes."

More about Jean O'Neill

Jean O'Neill is vice president channel for Cyxtera Technologies (cyxtera.com), a world-class infrastructure security organization. She is a talented leader with a proven track record of initiating and building partnerships with high-growth companies in the Managed Services Space. She is particularly effective at partnering with key stakeholders on both the company and the client side in driving alignment, growth strategies, solution development, pipeline acceleration, and account penetration with service integrators and ISV partners.

Jean also serves as a strategic advisory board director for SaaSMAX (saasmax.com). SaaSMAX is the value-add SaaS Marketplace and SaaS distributor that matches business cloud software vendors ("SaaS Vendors") and solution providers ("SaaS Resellers"), enabling both to create new revenues and partner opportunities. SaaSMAX also recently launched PartnerOptimizer, a sophisticated proprietary business intelligence platform for identifying and profiling channel partners.

Before joining Cyxtera, Jean held several executive positions for companies including Involta, Dynatrace, Terremark (a Verizon company), and Rackspace, among others. She graduated magna cum laude with a bachelor of science degree in communications from Kennesaw State University in Georgia.

Jean currently is an active member of the Alliance of Channel Women (allianceofchannelwomen.org), Cloud Girls (cloudgirls.org), and the San Diego chapter of Women in Technology (womenintechnology.org). She also regularly volunteers for other nonprofits in her hometown of San Diego, California.

Follow Jean on LinkedIn (Jean O'Neill) and Twitter (jeanoneill). She can also be contacted at joneill@mindspring.com.

CHAPTER 4 _____

A Conversation with Wendy L. Williams

Product Manager, Private Cloud and Security Services at INAP (inap.com)

Should is a futile word. It's about what didn't happen.
It belongs in a parallel universe. It belongs in another
dimension of space.
—Margaret Atwood, Canadian poet, novelist,
literary critic, essayist, inventor, teacher and
environmental activist (quote originally shared in her
book *The Blind Assassin*)

The possibilities far outweigh the disappointments.
Keep learning, keep believing, and keep seeking.
—Lailah Gifty Akita, author of *Think Great* and founder of
Smart Youth Volunteers Foundation

First, a Few of My Thoughts

I like to set intentions for my day—professional and personal. Today, one of my professional intentions was to begin writing this chapter featuring Wendy L. Williams. Last night, I re-read my notes from my wonderful interview with Wendy and went to sleep to let the interview marinate overnight. When I woke up, I had a sense that I wanted to share some of my thoughts with you on what happens when you feel "should on." I know this idea popped up for me because of one story in particular that Wendy shared. Stay tuned—it's a good one.

The next thing that happened blew my mind. Before I went into my office that morning to write, I happened to see a news clip reporting that the Golden Knights were in the Stanley Cup playoffs. The Golden Knights? I had no idea who they were. Over the years I had heard of several other new NHL franchises but never the Golden Knights. I investigated further to find the Golden Knights play for Las Vegas, and, in addition to celebrating going to the NHL finals, they were also celebrating their inaugural year. A professional sports franchisee making it to the "big game" in their first year of existence is virtually unheard of. I thought that was pretty darn cool.

As I continued my research, I learned that the Golden Knights bonded with their fans after the horrific Las Vegas mass shooting. Together, the Golden Knights and the city forged a connection that spoke to the very best qualities of being human. The story of the Knights' ascent during their first season was the story of a shaken city's rise from unimaginable pain. But here's where the mind-blowing moment came. As I read on, I learned there were a group of vocal critics who were not happy about the team's success. I was stunned. Why on Earth would someone who lived in the city of a successful sports team not be happy for that team's success? As these critics put it—the Golden Knights *should not* make it in their first year. They *should* have struggled first before finding success.

If I needed further validation that the universe wanted me to share my ideas of "shoulding" with you, I just received the nod I needed. These critics "shoulded on" the Golden Knights and their fans. And, I do know from experience that when you get "should on," it doesn't feel good. You just feel "shouldy."

This whole notion of the poisonous energy of "shoulding" has been a favorite topic of human potential teachers and life coaches for as long as I can remember. The psychologist Clayton Barbeau coined the term "shoulding yourself" (which he admits was inspired by another), to describe a cognitive distortion that occurs when you use the word "should." According to Barbeau, when you say you "should" do something, you're telling yourself you have an obligation to do something different from what you're actually doing. And with that comes one of my least favorite emotions—guilt. From my personal knowledge, as well as my work as a business and life coach, I can tell you that guilt doesn't feel positive to anyone. It's one of the lowest-vibrating human emotions.

Throughout my career, I have "should upon myself" many times. Usually when I say I "should" do something, it's something I don't particularly want to do or believe is the best thing for me to do. It's usually something that society, someone other than me, thinks I should do. When I operate from a "place of should," it just doesn't feel right or go well for me.

Sure, there are times when you do something that you should do but really don't want to do. You do it. It's not a big deal, and you move on. But for the big stuff in your life, pay attention. If you're "shoulding on yourself," and it's in an area of life that's really important to you, stop. For example, mid-way through my career I "shoulded myself" into staying in a job that was killing my soul (I know this sounds melodramatic, but I felt a part of me was dying off every day I stayed in that role). I told myself I should be grateful for making good money that allowed me to take care of my family (my daughter was around two years old and my husband was working for a family business that was barely above water). I told myself I should be thankful that I worked with such amazing colleagues (which I was) and that I should just suck it up. But at what cost? And who was to say that leaving that job couldn't turn into something better? It did.

The other thing to be wary of is when someone "shoulds" on you, as our Golden Knight "shoulders" did. Most people who "should on" others are judging based on their own beliefs and not on what they know to be true for someone else. And it's just as bad for you as "shoulding on yourself." For Wendy, our chapter focus, this occurred early in her career when a senior executive she worked with at a bank provided feedback on what career track she *should* pursue—and what career she *shouldn't* even dare to consider. I have to tell you that when she told me this story it rattled me, but how she responded to her experience told me a lot about Wendy. This is a very thoughtful, smart, and dignified woman who offers us sound advice on a wide range of topics from how to keep your career fresh and your contributions relevant through lifelong learning, to how you can involve your family in your career and develop their understanding of what you do for a living and how it contributes to the greater good of the family. I know you'll find tremendous value in reading what Wendy has to share.

Wendy L. Williams had a rather unconventional childhood compared to others her age growing up in the 1980s. Her mother earned a master's degree from Northwestern University in Chicago and had a successful career. Her father was a pharmacist who owned his own business. "There was no question whether or not my older brother and I were going to college," remembers Wendy. "We were raised to focus on our education, get a good job after college, move out of the house, and be productive adults."

> **My kids grew up seeing me have a career, and we talked about what that meant."**

Wendy saw, firsthand, how to be a woman in business in a way that resonated with her. "My mom and dad were excellent role models. Mom worked full time and had support within the house, and Dad owned a business. Our caregiver, who was more like a grandmother, was always there to greet us when we came home from school when we were young. My daughter and stepson were socialized in a similar way with both parents working full time. Their father had a flexible work schedule, allowing him to be available to take the children to school in the morning and enabling me to meet my commitments for early morning meetings. My kids grew up seeing me have a career, and we talked about what that meant."

Wendy learned other valuable lessons from her parents. Both her mother and father would regularly share stories from work. They would describe what happened with an employee and how they managed interactions. They would talk about business decisions they made throughout their day. This helped Wendy and her brother get a sense of workplace dynamics, which was further reinforced through real-life experiences working weekends at their father's drugstore.

Wendy also benefitted from her mother's ability to expertly connect life lessons through school- and work-related themes. "My mother's nature was to teach, and I share that nature as well," she notes. "As my daughter was growing up, I would ask her how her school day went. I'd listen to her, and we'd exchange stories. As she got older, I made it an ongoing practice to talk to her about my job as well—the good things that happened and the challenges—and to seek her input. In the course of our conversation I would say 'let me tell you something funny that happened to me at work today, I had a curveball question that came my way.' I'd then tell her the question and ask her how she would address it, rather than just tell her how I would or what I did."

Wendy believes that it's vital for women to overcommunicate with family because they are a part of your journey and will be making some sacrifices as well. She suggests that women take the time to make sure family members understand why your career is important, not just to you, but to them. As Wendy sees it, "You are also teaching your daughters and sons what it's like to be you. They get to see you in another dimension beyond 'mom.' And your husband gets to see you in another dimension beyond his wife and mother of his children. It expands the prism through which they view not just you, but all women. Where are they going to learn that, if you don't teach them?"

❝❝ When I took those programming classes, that's when my inner nerd was released!"

Wendy's formative years prepared her for success in college and beyond. She earned a bachelor of science degree in business from University of Illinois. She did well in her finance and economics classes in addition to classes in her marketing major, and she found she was attracted to technology as well. Rather than a more traditional language requirement, the university allowed students to take computer programming classes to satisfy the foreign language requirement. Wendy was quick to take advantage of this option. "When I took those programming classes, that's when my inner nerd was released!" laughs Wendy. "I started in tech before the personal computer. It was all mainframe at the time."

Wendy's exceptional grade point average, unique coursework, and leadership experience (she was the president of the university's Minority Business Student Association in the College of Business), attracted the attention of one of the largest banks in Chicago. Upon graduation, she was not only offered a job but also an opportunity to participate in an eighteen-month management-training program that exposed her to a wide range of career paths in banking. Shortly after taking the banking position, she was exposed to both racism and sexism in the workplace.

" They were shocked and made it clear that was not the department an African American should pick. But I picked it anyway."

"As I was going through the eighteen-month training rotation, I thought it would be cool to be in sales working in the bank's treasury department," shares Wendy. "I expressed my interest with the executives who managed the program. They were shocked and made it clear that was not the department an African American should pick. But I picked it anyway. As I began working there, I learned more about investment sales practices at the bank. At the time, the bank was not sponsoring women to take their Series 7 brokerage exam. You could not go through the coursework and licensing process without this sponsorship. Everything women sold for the bank went to a house account, and they were not paid commissions. Men, on the other hand, did not have these restrictions and were allowed to take the exam and, upon passing the exam, be paid full commissions."

In the end, while Wendy thought she could overcome the discrimination at the bank, she had an important realization—working with other people's money, selling municipal bonds and commercial paper all day long, wasn't the type of contribution she wanted to make to society. She felt a void. She wanted to be a part of something and to create something meaningful. As luck would have it, IBM was recruiting at the time and offered her a job as a mainframe systems engineer and advanced function printing specialist. She loved it and worked there until IBM spun off their printing division to Lexmark. She was a founding member of Lexmark, and then Hewlett Packard recruited her to run a corporate and enterprise sales territory in Chicago, selling their printing solutions. Her scope of responsibilities continued to increase with HP as, in her words, she "crossed the Rubicon from hardware to services." In this capacity she worked closely with the team responsible for developing cloud services in multiple data centers around the globe. It was an exciting time for Wendy.

After years of working with mega global IT companies, in 2016 Wendy found herself without a job when her company shed thousands of workers in an organization-wide reinvention and a series of divisional spin-offs. While most of her colleagues sought positions at other similarly large tech firms, Wendy made a bold choice to take her skills to SingleHop—a small, privately held managed cloud services provider that had recently been acquired by INAP.

Today, Wendy no longer has a team of thirty-five IT professionals at her beck and call, but she is very pleased with the path she took. "It would have been easier for me to go to another global tech giant where I would work with another large team, but I was looking for a different experience. I didn't want to blend my skills into a large organization again. I wanted to make more of an impact on the business and brush up on my technical acumen." She was also very attracted to the rough-and-tumble speed, spirit of entrepreneurism, and openness to new ideas that define SingleHop's culture. Another plus is that she enjoys greater diversity in her work projects with even more opportunities to contribute to her clients' success.

"Just the notion of providing customers with innovative, highly automated cloud-based solutions that provide them with a superior customer experience that also solves some of their most challenging business problems is very gratifying," finds Wendy. "We are literally making something together. I love the sausage-making aspect of working with brilliant software developers and architects, specifying what I need the service to do, working with them as they build it, and then seeing it come out of the oven into the customer's hands."

As Wendy reflects back on her long career, she offers other women several observations and recommendations. "As a woman of color and as a working mother, I experienced both overt and more subtle gender bias and discrimination," she notes. "The bar is always higher for less compensation, and we have to be perfect all of the time. There's less room for error than men are allowed. I also found that there is a limited support system to provide sponsorship."

> **I would get the question 'You have the temerity to ask for an SVP mentor?' and I'd answer 'Yes, I do have the temerity to ask for an SVP mentor. Why not? Because they are the ones who know what I want to know.'"**

On the topic of having others sponsor you and your work for career advancement consideration, Wendy offers up worthy advice. She found that the way to get promotions and plum assignments is to forge ahead to create your own career choices rather than wait for someone else to bring them to you. She would aggressively network two levels up, across, and down in the organization. She made sure that she was never isolated by her first-level manager and actively worked to cultivate and maintain both formal and informal mentors.

"I had a rule when it came to formal mentors—they had to be at least a senior vice president," Wendy asserts. "I would get the question 'You have the temerity to ask for an SVP mentor?' and I'd answer 'Yes, I do have the temerity to ask for an SVP mentor. Why not? Because they are the ones who know what I want to know. They are the ones who know where the puck is going and in what areas the company is investing.'"

Wendy was fortunate enough to have had several supportive managers over the course of her career. One woman in particular, Pamela, invested time to ensure Wendy's successful transition from a regional sales role to a global business development function. But Wendy observed that most of her colleagues did not have managers who exhibited this level of passion and expertise when it came to developing their own team. Wendy found that many managers were either interested in developing their people but didn't have the skills, or they were only interested in moving their own careers forward.

"Even if your manager is not interested in or doesn't have the capabilities to mentor you, you can still get the support you need," Wendy points out. "You need to identify the person you want to be your mentor, and then ask your manager to introduce you to that person and request that they consider a mentoring relationship with you. Your manager doesn't even have to make an in-person introduction—an email introduction works just fine. You must take the bull by the horns and ask your manager to do this for you. It's a part of her or his job to help you in your career development."

"And if your manager, for one reason or another, won't support your request, make a mental note of that, and extend your network. Again, it's important to not be isolated by your immediate manager. If he or she won't make the introduction, find someone who will."

Wendy has also found it beneficial to distinguish formal mentors from informal mentors. From her experience, formal mentorships work best when you put your mentor to work for you. For example, she would do dry runs of her presentations or share executive summaries of her research with her formal mentors. She would ask them for their feedback and to help fine-tune her work. "Chit chat" is not what she did with her formal mentors. There was always a very specific purpose or goal to her mentoring sessions. On the other hand, she was more inclined to have free-flowing conversations with informal mentors.

Another communication strategy Wendy recommends, which she found to be fruitful in her own career, is to keep people well informed. "As a woman, especially in tech, you must constantly lobby for your point of view and keep people on board. There are a million things people can invest in, but resources (money, people, time) are finite, so you really have to be clear on making your case and then continue to make your case over and over again. And you have to communicate regularly throughout the duration of a project to keep people with you in order to get your desired outcome."

❝❝ When you get that type of objection, you've got to press on or you've got to yield if someone presents a better idea."

Wendy believes that one of the reasons women tend to struggle in keeping others informed is that most either don't spend enough time on the tasks necessary and/or they don't possess the confidence required to be successful. "One of the things I tell myself is to ignore the voice that tells you that you can't do something, even if it's your own," she shares. "There will always be somebody who reacts to you in a way that signals 'you can't do this.' When you get that type of objection, you've got to press on or you've got to yield if someone presents a better idea. Typically, we cave in too quickly, because we are used to acquiescing. Don't."

"Conversely, being tenacious can be a strength, but you have to know when to yield," continues Wendy. "You've got to learn to take criticism and refine your thinking, because there is always going to be someone who knows more than you or has a better idea. It's better to join forces with that person and incorporate their thinking to make what you're bringing to the table even better. I don't take that as a negative trait. I take that as a positive one."

Wendy reminds us all to master our skills, stay sharp, and keep a fresh outlook. Regarding skill mastery, Wendy stresses the importance of becoming a subject matter expert in a strategic area. Be a go-to person for others. Wendy has a talent for strategic planning and research, which she continues to perfect. Throughout her career, she has been called upon to conduct industry scans where she would look across the industry, examine the company's routes to market, and make recommendations based on revenue potential, among other factors. She became known for possessing this skill set.

Furthermore, to stay sharp, Wendy encourages women to find the time to do their homework. "You have to invest time to figure out where the bus is going in your company. Whether it's the Internet of Things, machine learning, block chain, artificial intelligence, whatever the new buzzword or application, make it your priority to master those skills."

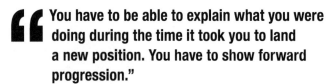

You have to be able to explain what you were doing during the time it took you to land a new position. You have to show forward progression."

Even though Wendy stays on top of most industry changes, there are times when the world of IT is moving so quickly she can feel stagnant. When this feeling strikes, it's time to expand her skill set. On one occasion she had a gap of nine months between jobs and wanted to make sure she accounted for that gap. What did she do? In addition to keeping her skills sharp by taking on pro bono consulting assignments, she received her Internet of Things (IofT) Certification from Massachusetts Institute of Technology (MIT). "You have to be able to explain what you were doing during the time it took you to land a new position," recommends Wendy. "You have to show forward progression."

Lastly, Wendy recommends seeking out work-related groups, seminars, and workshops to continue to learn about industry developments and to surround yourself with people who are going where you want to go. "It's great to have those girlfriends who you have lunch and shop with, but remember, as one of my managers once told me 'iron sharpens iron,'" Wendy says. "Surround yourself with people who are smarter than you, who convey a level of enthusiasm and passion for tech. Keep your resume and LinkedIn profile updated. And connect with the people you meet—have coffee with them. You never know who knows who you need to know."

More about Wendy L. Williams

Wendy L. Williams serves as product manager for private cloud and security services at Internap Corporation (INAP). INAP is a provider of high-performance internet infrastructure including colocation, managed services and hosting, cloud, and high-performance network services (inap.com). Throughout her extensive career, Wendy has made significant contributions to large global IT organizations, including twenty years with Hewlett Packard (HP) and eleven years with IBM/Lexmark, as well as a smaller, privately held firm, SingleHop, which was acquired by INAP in March of 2018.

Wendy has earned a reputation for being a self-motivated global product manager and channel sales leader who has been consistently promoted to take on the most complex, strategic initiatives. She has a proven track record of successful strategy creation and execution in sustaining mature product lines, innovating new ones, and driving transformational go-to-market initiatives with sales teams, channel, and alliance partners. Her top areas of software and services expertise include: ERP, Traditional IT, Mainframe, Public, Private, Hybrid Clouds, IaaS, PaaS, SaaS, and IoT.

A graduate from the University of Illinois with a bachelor of science degree in business, Wendy served as president for the university's College of Business Administration Minority Students Association. Moreover, her belief in lifelong learning has resulted in numerous postcollege professional certifications. Her most recent education accomplishment was an Internet of Things certification in 2017 from MIT.

In her personal life, Wendy enjoys spending time with her two adult children, daughter Pilar and son Jordan. Wendy is an active volunteer who donates consulting time to promote economic growth and empowerment for nonprofits served by the Chatman Lewis Flaggs Consulting Group. She also serves as a mentor to students at Proviso East High School in Maywood, Illinois. Wendy loves all things tech and is a lifelong learner, an avid reader, artist, and chef.

Follow Wendy on LinkedIn (Wendy Williams). She can also be contacted at wwilliams@inap.com.

CHAPTER 5 _____

A Conversation with Monica Morrison

Manager, ITSM Process Improvement at a major health insurance
company in Maryland

It is literally true that you can succeed best and quickest
by helping others to succeed.
—Napoleon Hill, author

The best way to find yourself is to lose yourself in the
service of others.
—Mahatma Gandhi, civil rights leader

First, a Few of My Thoughts

I am a big fan of anyone who demonstrates an average or (even
better yet) above-average use of emotional intelligence at work.
It brings me great glee. I'm going to talk about this in greater
depth in the second part of this book. Get ready.

For now, a good (and simple) working definition for emotional
intelligence, which is often referred to as EI or EQ (emotional
quotient), is this: someone who is emotionally intelligent is
someone who relates well to others, works well with others, and
effectively manages their own emotions each and every day.

Monica believes that to be successful in technology, you
really have to have a strong connection with people and genuine
interest in supporting their IT needs. She notes this is especially
critical if you're working closely with internal and external clients.
She understands emotional intelligence.

When she shared her philosophy with me, I had to laugh. Not because I disagreed with her—oh no, I enthusiastically agreed with her! Her thoughts reminded me of an IT resource I knew several years ago who would tell everyone who was willing to listen that he liked computers more than people—and he was the company's primary IT go-to person. After he parted ways with the company and we were interviewing to replace his position, we found a candidate who had the skill set *and* the desire to serve others. She loved working in tech support, and the team loved her right back. It was such a different dynamic. The new tech resource lifted the energy of the entire company with her willingness to assist others no matter how simple or complex the request, break issues down into easy-to-understand concepts and words, and put forth a genuine effort to make life a bit easier for end users who were struggling with system outages or their own user errors.

This is yet another example of where women can shine in technology. Many women have developed their emotional intelligence in ways that create distinct competitive advantages for their companies. And people enjoy working with emotionally intelligent people who get the job done.

There is one last thing I wanted to tell you about Monica before we dive into her chapter. She was the very first woman to respond to my LinkedIn invitation to participate in this book project. When we initially spoke, it was clear to me that Monica connected to the spirit and mission of the book. She has a great passion for advancing women in technology, which shines through clearly in her story. She's not afraid to share her past struggles and the lessons she's learned along the way.

Grab your favorite beverage, sit back, and enjoy reading what she has to say.

"If you're thinking about a career in tech, make sure you are truly passionate about technology and not just looking for an easy way to make money," suggests Monica. "And never, ever forget that this is a service industry."

Monica continues, "Many technology professionals don't 'get' the service aspect of technology, especially if they're not on the frontlines. It really doesn't matter what you're doing in technology, be it security, networking, programming, you name it; ultimately, you're engaged in providing a service to others. We're all in the service business."

Monica started her career in technology in the early nineties. She had a natural talent for working with the business applications available at the time—Word Perfect; Lotus 1, 2, 3; and Harvard Graphics, among others. She became a super user who trained others on how to optimize their reports and presentations. She was working in meetings and convention planning for a large international trade association. And though she felt she had a promising future in that industry, she really enjoyed working with technology.

Monica became excited about pursuing a career in IT when a new position became available in the company. She shared her interest with the IT director but was told he could only bring someone in who had prior IT experience. She was not deterred. She continued to provide office tech support to her colleagues who asked for her assistance.

Less than a year later the company hired a new vice president. He did an organization-wide review of teams that reported to him to assess the skills and interests of the staff.

When he met with Monica's manager, who was the director of meetings and conventions, she mentioned that Monica was a natural with computers. That meeting led to Monica being offered the IT position that she had originally applied for with the IT director.

"It was ironic that the same position I was denied was actually handed to me less than a year later," Monica relates. "It was a wonderful opportunity that I am still very grateful for. That experience launched my IT career, and that's one of the reasons I'm such a big proponent of helping others."

> ❝❝ **Many women in tech have to work harder than their male counterparts to gain credibility. People hold assumptions that we're not as good as or as technical as men."**

As Monica's career evolved, the way she assisted others evolved as well. Initially she found great satisfaction helping people solve technical issues. "The first joy for me was feeling that sense of accomplishment that came from figuring out technical problems. It's no secret that people can get extremely frustrated when they can't get their work done on their computers. It felt good to help them get back to work, be productive, and feel at peace again."

She then transitioned into management and was able to help people in other ways. A natural leader and teacher, Monica became a sought-after mentor who looked for ways to give others an opportunity to grow and be recognized.

"When I was a director of IT, one of my technicians was trying to solve an issue with a network printer," remembers Monica. "He had been spinning his wheels for a few days when I realized he had not received the proper escalation support. Although I was well beyond my hands-on troubleshooting days, as his manager, I felt I needed to help him. I was able to quickly figure out and resolve the issue. Afterwards I printed some information, called the technician into my office, and showed him a small detail that he could check for in the future that would allow him to fix the issue, and those similar to it, in five minutes or less. Of course, he was relieved and happy to have the issue resolved and to have learned a new troubleshooting technique. What sticks with me the most is what happened next. One of my colleagues overheard the exchange, came into my office and said, 'The way you explained that to him was so courteous and professional. You are a really great mentor.' Throughout my career I have tried to use every opportunity to impart knowledge to others to help them grow. I'm still in touch with that young man, and he continues to soar in his IT career."

When Monica started a position managing her company's desktop support and service desk teams, one of the first things she did was schedule time to meet with each technician. She wanted to assess their skills as well as interests. In particular, she remembers assessing a young woman who worked on the service desk and was immediately impressed with the woman's organizational skills, attention to detail, and excellent customer service. Monica thought she would be a great fit for a newly created position and asked the woman if she'd be interested in applying, which she was. Monica had no hesitation in promoting the young woman and continues to mentor her today.

Monica recalled another pivotal hire she made in her career when her department was undergoing an extensive expansion and she was hiring several positions. A young man who worked in the mailroom applied for a service desk position. He didn't have any IT experience but had helped out with office moves by pitching in to disassemble and reassemble computers. Monica wanted to give him a chance.

"He came highly recommended, knew our ticketing system, and had great customer service skills," notes Monica. "I sought out the opinions of a core group of individuals this young man would be supporting as well as my mentor at the time. They affirmed my desire to give him a chance. I gave him the opportunity to join our IT department and he absolutely shined. He did a fantastic job and since has been promoted. To do for him what someone else had done for me brought me yet another level of personal and professional satisfaction."

In addition to finding enjoyment in being of service to others, Monica feels strongly that to be a successful woman in tech you have to develop your confidence and assertiveness. "We have to be confident in ourselves," she believes. "Many women in tech have to work harder than their male counterparts to gain credibility. People hold assumptions that we're not as good as or as technical as men."

Monica remembers several instances when her abilities were less valued for no other reason than the fact that the final two chromosomes in her DNA strand are XX. "Early on, it wasn't even a question of whether or not I was as good as my male counterparts," she states. "The response was no, definitely not. She's female."

> **Of all the negative speak we may hear from others concerning their perceptions of our abilities, the voice that can do the most damage to our confidence, and in turn our ultimate success, is our own."**

"After years of building my credibility and being a top performer, I became a manager. You'd think that the position would come with a certain degree of respect and recognition that I was technically adept. Wrong again. I've had a number of male subordinates question my technical guidance. I remember an occasion where a male subordinate was continuing to refute the guidance I was giving him on how to build a server. I literally had to search through my files and pull out a document I had previously used to build a server to prove to him that what I was saying was indeed correct. Men in technology don't have to prove themselves, they are automatically given credibility, which is not always the case with women."

"Most women have to regularly prove themselves. As women, many times we have to overcome doubt, silence naysayers, and overturn stereotypes by proving our knowledge, skills, and abilities. But I've learned along the way that the only person you need to prove yourself to is you. And you need to do that from the start. You need to be careful not to buy in to stereotypes or believe the myth that women aren't as good as men in technology roles. Of all the negative speak we may hear from others concerning their *perceptions* of our abilities, the voice that can do the most damage to our confidence, and in turn our ultimate success, is our own. Take it from someone who at one time listened to and internalized those negative stereotypes but who ultimately overcame them: you have to *know* your value and what you bring to the table. Once you know who *you* are, your confidence will soar."

When Monica realized that she wasn't any less capable than her male counterparts, she actually found that she was better than many of them. It wasn't just that her attention to detail and her organizational, interpersonal, and communication skills were superior, but in many cases her technical skills were more advanced as well.

"To be honest, in many of the organizations I've worked for, I've seen women far outshine men in technical positions," shares Monica. "Don't get me wrong, I'm not saying that women are hands-down better than men in technology positions. I would never make an unfounded, unresearched statement such as that. However, what I am saying is that in my experience I have observed that many women in technology approach their roles much like women have approached the roles of child-bearer, mother, nurturer, house manager, diplomat, accountant, and the like for centuries without even leaving the home. That is, with a keen attention to detail, a selfless sense of commitment, a warm communication style, a graceful resilience, a quiet humility, a remarkable ability to multitask, a sincere compassion for others, and an unrelenting desire to excel that make them extraordinary. In short, women in technology rock!"

Another must-have for women in tech today is assertiveness. As Monica sees it, you have to know what talents you bring to the table, know how to articulate your personal brand, and not be afraid to speak up. She shared a story that resonated with her from a Microsoft conference she attended in 2012. It was a story of a talented, hard-working woman at a tech company. Many mornings as she headed into work, she found herself riding in the elevator with the CEO. She was too afraid to not say anything to the CEO, but she didn't know what to say, so she would talk about the weather. When her male counterparts got in the elevator, they easily struck up conversations with the CEO by talking about what they were doing in their departments.

What do you think happened when the company was looking for people to promote? The CEO approved the promotions of the men who promoted their work while riding in the elevator. Sadly, the "weather girl" was looked over, even though she was among the most talented professionals in the company.

 Make sure that your accomplishments have your name and face attached to them. Put simply, make sure you get credit for what you do."

"I took that story to heart," says Monica. "I had been the weather girl in the past and made a point to change that. Some time after that conference, when I found myself in the elevator with our company's chief information officer, I asserted myself and spoke about a new process our IT Service Desk team had implemented. He said he was impressed and showed a genuine interest in what I shared. It didn't come naturally to me at first, but I took an important step that day in being assertive. I continue to make it a point to talk about accomplishments when speaking to senior leaders as opposed to the weather."

Monica also reminds women to be assertive right away and not to wait to initiate conversations with senior and C-level executives. "There was a gentleman I managed who had a very good relationship with the company's CEO. I didn't have my first conversation with the CEO until I had been there for nearly two years. This other manager, my subordinate, knew the CEO on a first-name basis, and I didn't. I realized that I was so preoccupied with the job at hand that I wasn't taking time to build my personal brand. Ladies, don't miss opportunities to brand yourselves. Your brand is you, and you are your brand. Make sure that your accomplishments have your name and face attached to them. Put simply, make sure you get credit for what you do."

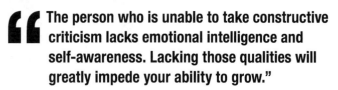 **The person who is unable to take constructive criticism lacks emotional intelligence and self-awareness. Lacking those qualities will greatly impede your ability to grow."**

Another attribute that Monica has found to be just as important as confidence and assertiveness is humility. "The humble person is the one who will eventually be great because the humble person knows how to take advice and constructive feedback and make themselves better. When someone says something disparaging about her or his work, the humble person doesn't take it personally. She or he takes that as a cue to improve and create a better experience for that person the next time."

Monica remembers a couple times in her career where someone shared negative feedback with her. Each time that happened to her, she thanked the person and made a vow to herself that she would turn the experience around so that one day that person would commend her or her team's work. And that's exactly what happened. Monica had been appointed a leadership role overseeing her company's service desk operation and was told by a team of managers that the department was horrible. "I sat in on a series of meetings where I listened to them rant about how poor the performance had been," retells Monica. "Their complaints were valid, and I reassured them that I would take their feedback seriously. I also vowed to myself that these managers would one day praise the service desk for our excellent work. With much hard work, we turned the operation around, and within six months those managers were publicly praising our accomplishments."

Monica has seen what happens when people have a hard time accepting constructive feedback, and she cautions us all that if we become too haughty or high-minded to accept constructive criticism, we will never be able to improve. "The person who is unable to take constructive criticism lacks emotional intelligence and self-awareness. Lacking those qualities will greatly impede your ability to grow. On the flip side, the person who is aware of their weaknesses as well as strengths and is humble enough to take feedback, look at themselves honestly, and make changes as needed, will continue to improve themselves. That's how you advance from good to great."

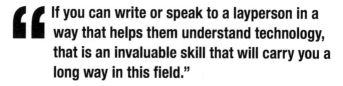

If you can write or speak to a layperson in a way that helps them understand technology, that is an invaluable skill that will carry you a long way in this field."

On the topic of training and professional development, Monica echoes the advice shared by other women in this book—stay on top of trends, educate yourself, and be flexible and adaptable so that you can keep pace with constant change and innovation. "Be willing to reinvent yourself," she reminds. "I've reinvented myself several times throughout my IT career, and if technology continues to change and evolve, as I know it will, I see a few more reinventions yet to come".

She also stresses the importance of cultivating your communication skills. "The reality is that many technology professionals are not good communicators, not verbally or in writing," notes Monica. "It's common to read communications from the IT department that are overly technical, filled with jargon and complicated phrases that mean nothing to most internal and external customers. If you can write or speak to a layperson in a way that helps them understand technology, that is an invaluable skill that will carry you a long way in this field."

Finally, Monica gives advice for breaking through the glass ceiling. "We need to talk about what we want, what matters to us. There was a time when I felt I really deserved a promotion. I wanted it and thought I was going to get it. The promotion never materialized, and for that I accept part of the blame."

Monica's manager at the time had talked about promoting her at some point in the future (she was only six months into her position). Instead of checking in with her manager on a regular basis to see how she was doing and ask what she could do further to be considered for a promotion, she didn't. At her annual reviews, her manager expressed to her that she was doing a great job and that she was highly skilled. At one review he also gave her a piece of insight—people at the top don't know you.

"It ties back to the need to be assertive and not assume that just because you do a great job you'll be recognized," Monica finds. "I think back to the two years it took me to have a conversation with my CEO. That was two years of phenomenal work that was done with no name or face attached to it except those of my superiors. Women, especially, have a tendency to get comfortable working beneath others and letting others take credit for their work. Don't settle for that. It is so important for us to get out in front of what we are doing and make ourselves known. I'll say it again, your brand is you, and you are your brand. Make sure the movers and shakers know who you are—and make sure that who you are is *not* the weather girl!"

More about Monica Morrison

Monica Morrison is manager, ITSM process improvement at a major health insurance company in Maryland. She is a dynamic, passionate leader with remarkable strategic vision and focus on customer satisfaction, process improvement, and solutions implementation. Monica has more than twenty years of experience implementing ITSM best practices that have improved service delivery and support in large companies as well as nonprofit organizations. She has extensive experience coaching and mentoring individuals and building strong, cohesive teams that achieve results.

Before signing on with her present employer in 2017, she served as senior manager, IT service and support for Inovalon (Bowie, MD) and senior management consultant for The Brookings Institution (Washington, DC), among other IT leadership roles. She is ITIL and HDI certified.

Monica is also a published author and popular industry presenter. She is presenting at HDI 2019 on the topic "Next Stop Quality: 5 Steps to Increase Service Desk Effectiveness." Her article on the same subject appeared recently in HDI's *SupportWorld*. She was the FUSiON18 Conference track chairperson for the Capitalizing on Your Service Management Investment track and presented at FUSiON17 on the topic of "Service Desk Evolution: From Underperforming to High-Performing in 180 Days." Her article covering the same topic was also published in *SupportWorld*. She is a member of HDI, iTSMF, and Women in Technology. She is actively involved with the Capital Area chapter of HDI where she serves as the Vice President of Program Logistics. She also volunteers her time speaking to youths entering the IT field at the Hope Project, a Washington, DC, nonprofit organization that provides IT training and development to young adults.

Follow Monica on LinkedIn (Monica Morrison). She can also be contacted at monicamd_2000@yahoo.com.

CHAPTER 6

A Conversation with Tina Gravel

Senior Vice President Global Channels at Cyxtera (cyxtera.com)

> Someone once told me not to be afraid of being
> afraid, because, as she said, "Anxiety is a glimpse
> of your own daring." Isn't that great? It means
> that part of your agitation is just excitement about
> what you're getting ready to accomplish. Don't
> sell yourself short by being so afraid of failure that
> you don't dare to make any mistakes. Make your
> mistakes and learn from them.
> —Maria Shriver, journalist

First, a Few of My Thoughts

Wow! When I first talked to Tina Gravel, she took my breath away. Her vibrancy and passion knocked me back a couple of steps, and then she disarmed me with an exceedingly high-level of honesty about her own operating style and lessons learned. Tina's candor is quite rare…and very appealing.

It was also no surprise to me that Tina is quite the salesperson. Her sales abilities and success in selling and launching new businesses is extraordinary. She is one of the few women I've seen described by others as an "award-winning" executive. Tina's awards speak to a long career of impressive accomplishments. Earlier in her career she was named a top ten "Women in Black" recipient, an honor given by the City of Chicago and *istreet* magazine, which recognized her leadership in the technology industry. Most recently she received the Cloud Girls "TrailBlazer Award" for her work in cloud computing (2017); was named one of the "Women in the Channel 2017" by CRN (a top news source for solution providers and the IT channel); was ranked #18 in CRN's "100 People You Don't Know but Should" list for her work with Cryptzone (2016); and was included in CRN's annual Top 50 "Women of the Channel" list for her successful work in the indirect channel and with alliances (2013).

But for all her of awards and accolades received, Tina admits that perhaps one of her greatest accomplishments was learning to be more self-aware. To this day she is very mindful of how her emotions affect her and others. She knows that emotional intelligence is not a given; it's something on which you have to consciously and continuously work. Amen, sister!

I have been an avid explorer and developer of EI for a number of decades, and I still find that it's one of the most difficult yet rewarding subjects to learn and apply. Whenever I start working with a company to help its leaders and employees develop EI, I tell them that they are very courageous to tackle the topic. Yes, courageous.

EI development is not for the faint of heart because it is exceptionally complex. There is no one "right" way to develop EI that works for all. EI development opportunities are *everywhere*. The possibilities for how EI can be demonstrated are limitless. There are few, if any, who can say they are EI masters. Ultimately, as Tina learned, EI is about becoming the boss of your own emotions and in the process tuning in to what really is important in life—what you value and treasure most.

The other thing I dig about Tina is that she does not cave in to fear. In the quote at the beginning of this chapter, Maria Shriver talks about how anxiety or agitation about something is often just excitement about what you're getting ready to accomplish. I have found that nugget of wisdom to be true over and over again in my career. There are times, to be sure, that fear is founded. You do need to heed that feeling. However, oftentimes the anxiety you're feeling is due to the simple fact that you're doing something new or something you think is going to be hard. Do it anyway!

I remember very early in my career I worked as a bank marketing coordinator. My boss was a seasoned VP of marketing who annually taught a three-hour marketing essentials class to a group of more than three hundred presidents and other bankers at a weeklong executive program sponsored by the Illinois Bankers Association (IBA). He had a last-minute schedule conflict and couldn't teach an upcoming session, so he asked me to do it for him. I was in my mid-twenties and new to banking and relatively new to marketing. Even though he told me he would give me all his preparatory notes and materials, I felt an incredibly high degree of stomach-churning anxiety. But I recognized the wonderful opportunity it was and told him I'd be happy to do it. I poured over the materials for hours upon hours and did numerous mock presentations in front of my husband, cat, and houseplants. Even as I'm writing this, I can still vividly feel the nauseating anxiousness I felt in my hotel room the sleepless night before the big event.

The next day, minutes before my session was scheduled to start, I was sitting in the back of the room when the previous speaker finished up and the facilitator introduced me. Nobody, to that point, had noticed me. When my name was announced, I just started introducing myself and sharing my prefacing comments as I was walking up the long aisle to get to the front of the standing-room only audience. I remember people turning around as I was walking up. Something came over me. Here I was, this twenty-something, sharing funny stories and shaking people's hands as my anxiety fell away. I had the time of my life. The following week the CEO of our bank received a note from the IBA thanking him for allowing me the time off to facilitate the session and letting him know that my presentation was the highest-rated session of the weeklong program—and by a large margin. Yes, indeed, anxiety certainly can be a glimpse of your own daring. It can lead to quite the adventure, and in my case, it turned out to be a career-changing adventure at that. Within three months of the IBA session, I was promoted and became an officer of the bank—and one of the first women in the organization to attain that title.

As you read this chapter featuring Tina, a number of themes will emerge to help you be more self-aware, more courageous, more willing to stretch your capabilities, more willing to learn new subjects, more comfortable in selling your strengths, and more determined to put yourself in the driver's seat of your own life. Truly, you are in for a treat here. Let's start off by exploring how Tina got into tech in the first place. It's quite the story!

Looking back to the 80s, 90s, and 00s, few women started their careers in tech with the intent to land a job working with a technology company. Most will tell you they "fell into" the field or entered into it in a rather circuitous fashion. Tina Gravel describes her path to tech as being "a very strange story."

"I took the majority of my college courses at Amherst College, although I graduated from University of Massachusetts. At the time, little ivies like Amherst didn't train people to go into a specific industry. The college focused on what you would become in life—a writer, a doctor, a lawyer, a businessperson. There was no discussion about a career in sales or technology."

Even though Tina had an early interest in technology (she worked in the Amherst College tech department cleaning tapes to learn more about the field), as she neared graduation, she wasn't quite sure what career path was best for her. She decided to apply to a few law schools and was accepted. "I paid for my first semester and was getting ready to go to law school while every little cell of my body was saying 'don't do it, you can't go forward with this,'" Tina recalls.

Tina honored her intuition and did not go to law school. She knew what she had to do next—get employed. She picked up the telephone and called the president of Mobil Chemical, a good friend's dad. "I told him, I'm not going to law school, I need a job, and I need your help," says Tina. "He was amazing. He wrote letters introducing me to other businesspeople and companies. He also happened to mention that from what he knew of me, he thought I would probably like sales."

That's exactly when the seed was planted that eventually led to Tina being in high-tech sales. She didn't see herself as a programmer, but she was excited about the idea of computers and wanted to be involved in some meaningful way. With her newfound career focus, she interviewed with IBM, Digital Equipment Corporation (DEC), and other companies that were considered to be "tech" companies at the time. Unfortunately, they did not return her interest.

In the meantime, Tina was offered a job made possible from that same friend who worked at Mobil Chemical and thought she could excel in sales. The offer, which she took, was not for a tech job though. The position entailed selling a new product that would revolutionize the supermarket industry and, in due course, every retail business on the planet—plastic shopping bags. At the time, no one had heard of plastic bags, and it was Tina's job to convince just about every grocery store on the east coast that plastic was the way to go. Not only did she sell the bags, her success was due in large part to how she sold them. "I had never touched a power tool in my life. I had to drill in the hardware to hold the bag rack, set the bag system up, and train the people on how to use the bags and how to overcome objections."

"I feel badly about it now because I feel responsible in a way for causing all these bags to be in the system," Tina admits. "I didn't know about the environmental consequences at the time." Her success selling plastic grocery bag systems in the East resulted in a promotion to lead her own sales territory one year after starting and a transfer to one of the company's largest markets—Chicago.

> ❝ I've had success, yes, but it's been really challenging, too. As soon as you know something, someone is going to move your cheese, and you're going to have to learn something else.❞

Once in Chicago, Tina felt the pull to the tech industry again. She went back to the people with whom she originally interviewed before she took the job with Mobil Chemical. She cold-called them, emailed them, and asked them for another interview opportunity. She had some sales experience under her belt and knew better how she could contribute to these companies. She received two job offers from the very same people who had once turned her down—IBM and DEC. Surprisingly, she ended up not taking either of the two offers. Why? Because her ability to take the initiative, move out of her comfort zone, and talk to strangers led to an even better job prospect.

"I was coming back from a business trip and stopped at a popular restaurant near O'Hare airport," remembers Tina. "I struck up a conversation with this gentleman who asked me about my work. I told him I had two job offers and was considering taking on a new position in tech with either IBM or DEC. And he says to me 'why haven't you interviewed with us?'"

Tina came to learn that "us" was McDonnell Douglas Automation (McAuto). She was surprised to learn that they were more than an aircraft company with a $500 million business in providing access cycles on their mainframes to other companies. They were engaged in technology. She was intrigued. During the interview she learned they had an excellent four-month training program where she would be trained to program and sell the company's software. Plus, they offered her a salary that was $7,000 more than what she was earning at the time with Mobil. No further arm-twisting was needed. She took the job.

Tina also learned she was part of a large Equal Employment Opportunity Commission (EEOC) mandated hiring effort to attract more women and other minorities to McDonnell Douglas. The four-month training program and subsequent onboarding process was intense. Of the twenty-six people who originally participated in her training class, only five were still with the company fewer than twenty-four months later. Tina was one of those five, and she thrived in the company's business environment. "I remember the president of McDonnell Douglas standing up on a stage at one of our achievement club award meetings," reflects Tina. "He pointed at me and said in front of the group 'this woman is making more than me this year.' I was the company's number-one salesperson, and I learned IT over time. I realized that I was pretty good at this type of work, but that had it not been for the EEOC, I would not have gotten in."

Once Tina landed in technology, she never left. Her love of learning led her to become an expert in selling cloud technologies and working with channel partners to teach them how to sell the cloud. She received promotion after promotion and moved nimbly from company to company during a series of mergers and acquisitions. "I've had success, yes, but it's been really challenging, too," she acknowledges. "As soon as you know something, someone is going to move your cheese, and you're going to have to learn something else. It never stops."

One recommendation Tina has for women already in tech, as well as those interested in a tech career, is to make it a point to ensure people know what you do and the effort you're putting into your work. You have to sell yourself. Constantly.

"Sometimes it's hard to be that direct," she recognizes. "You don't have to hit people over the head with your accomplishments. You can remind them of your projects during meetings when you socialize over the work the team is doing and your part in that. You can also update people on your endeavors when you ask for their support. There are a number of ways you can increase visibility for your efforts."

Fairly recently, Tina had a powerful reminder of the importance of promoting your work. One of her peers had taken over a project that she and her team had worked on for just over a year. Two weeks after she handed the project off to him, she was at a meeting where her colleague presented a written synopsis of the project status and what had been done. It included all the work that Tina and her team had completed over the previous year. "At first, I was floored," she retells. "The way he presented the update gave the impression that he was able to complete more work on the project in two weeks than I was able to complete in a year. Although I knew that was not true, others would not know that same truth. Plus, I couldn't very well say 'hey, those are all the tasks I did.' I'm not criticizing what my peer did, it just taught me a lesson that I can do better at communicating and writing about my work so others are kept informed."

> **You need to step into traffic a bit on the things that are important to you, even if you may not know them well, and then put in the time to learn more."**

Tina reminds women that if they don't promote themselves and their accomplishments, no one will. She recommends regularly reporting on and submitting project updates that are succinct and focus specifically on the actions you've taken. She also suggests the importance of encouraging others to connect with you if they need more information (that's the time to give them more details) or have feedback to share. Keep it simple and direct.

In addition to making it a top priority to sell or promote yourself, Tina also recommends that women need to get *uncomfortable*—they need to be able to put themselves and their ideas out into the world. "You need to step into traffic a bit on the things that are important to you, even if you may not know them well, and then put in the time to learn more," she asserts. "That kind of stretching and forcing yourself is the only way you're going to get ahead now. I don't think there is any other way."

❝❝ Bill told me that the way to get ahead is to talk to strangers and not be afraid to do so."

Tina knows a few things about getting out of your comfort zone. When she first started working for McDonnell Douglas, she was petrified that she would lose her job. She felt as if she was way out over her ski tips and lucky to have such a plum position. She would have done anything to keep it. She desperately wanted to be successful. She received some opportune and unsolicited advice from her boss at the time, Bill Schmidt, who has since passed.

"Bill told me that the way to get ahead is to talk to strangers and not be afraid to do so. He reminded me that I had a valuable service to share. He told me people will give me a hard time, so make a script. He told me to make twenty-five cold calls a day. And he told me that it's okay if people hang up on me because one day talking to strangers and making cold calls would pay off. It was the best advice that anyone gave me, and a few years later I thanked him. I was so grateful."

A few years later, Tina received some other advice that she hadn't necessarily sought out but which changed her professional career for the better. One day, she started up a conversation with a coworker on the Chicago subway and happened to tell him she was looking for ways to provide more value to her clients and move up in her company. He suggested she explore insurance software and gave her numerous reasons that would be a good move for her. As luck would have it, she had just heard of a new position that had opened up at McAuto selling insurance software. "So, I went into a bookstore and bought a book on insurance," Tina relates. "After I read the book, I marched into my boss's office and said 'I heard you're hiring someone to sell insurance software to our partners. I want to do that job.' He asked me, point blank, 'what makes you think you can do that job?' and I rattled off my newfound knowledge about underwriting, property casualty insurance, and other information I'd gained from reading that book. The biggest fear I had was of not being successful. If knowing about and selling insurance software to our partners was going to help me be successful, I was all in."

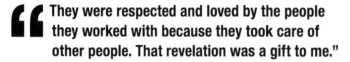 **They were respected and loved by the people they worked with because they took care of other people. That revelation was a gift to me."**

Tina got the job and discovered early on that the best seller of insurance software at the time was a man by the name of Billy Henderson in New York City. She wanted to know what he knew. Once again, motivated by the fear of not being successful in her new endeavor, she got the go-ahead from her boss to fly out to New York and spend a couple of days with Billy Henderson and his business partner. She was determined to learn what they did to be so fruitful in selling insurance software. Tina recounts, "What I learned from these guys was simply to be myself and never pretend to be anyone else. They really lived that advice. They didn't put on any airs, whatsoever. At times they were funny, sometimes even silly, and they were very smart. Their sales presentations conveyed exactly who they were and what was important to them. They were respected and loved by the people they worked with because they took care of other people. That revelation was a gift to me."

Another career revelation for Tina happened a number of years later. Often, the road to understanding and being who you are is not necessarily a smooth one. Even those who possess a clear idea of how they operate and what's important to them can be sidetracked, as Tina discovered. "A start-up tech company that knew of my sales successes approached me with a job opportunity to lead and manage their sales team. I had been a sales performer for most of my career and considered myself a neophyte in management. Although I was hesitant to accept the position, the executives with whom I interviewed encouraged me to take the leap."

"I decided that to be successful in my new sales management role I was going to train everyone who worked for me to be exactly like me!" Tina laughs. "That meant they were going to dress a certain way, talk a certain way, and function, in general, in a certain way. I was a complete micromanager. I was a monster. I was impossible to live with, and I was miserable."

"One day my boss said to me 'Tina, you're the number-one manager in the company, but your team doesn't like you. Can you imagine if they liked you how much harder they'd work for you?'" Tina noted that her boss coached her in a very respectful and nonemotional way, and she got the point. She realized that the road to management success was not paved with "mini me" employees who operated just like her.

Over the years, Tina continued to build her self-awareness. She participated in 360-degree-feedback analyses to understand how she affects others and herself. She found the discovery process to be of great value. Tina also found value in discovering the types of companies and projects that were the best fit for her. However, she gained much of this knowledge by experiencing an exceptionally painful time in her career.

> **When you go home from work day after day and find yourself crying, eating a box of cookies, and hearing from those close to you that what's happening at your place of employment 'doesn't sound right,' well, I'll tell you what, it isn't right for you."**

Tina knew she enjoyed working for companies that were flexible and could swiftly move to capitalize on new ideas and solutions that her clients needed. She also liked to grow into her role so people could see, over time, how she performed and contributed to the organization. This is what attracted her to work with start-ups and new divisions at larger companies. But she was always striving for more, and when she accepted a senior-level management role at a very large, more traditional organization, she found herself in what felt like another world—a world unlike anything she had experienced before.

"There were a lot of rules, and I stepped all over myself all day long," she notes. "Also, for the first time in my career, I experienced jealousy that was targeted at me because I held a top position and came into that position from the outside. The majority of the people I worked with didn't know me. They hadn't been able to see what I was able to do before taking the position, so they didn't readily see how I could contribute to the team."

Tina worked hard to prove her worth, but she admits it was a difficult year. "When you go home from work day after day and find yourself crying, eating a box of cookies, and hearing from those close to you that what's happening at your place of employment 'doesn't sound right,' well, I'll tell you what, it isn't right for you."

Within two days of leaving the company, Tina felt a huge weight was lifted from her. Her physical body changed. She was able to breathe again and decompress. She was no longer trying to force herself to fit into a company and culture that was not the right fit for her.

Tina reflects, "The lesson I learned from that experience is to cut your losses, get out, and move on. Don't try to hang in there, because the truth is you don't owe anybody anything. If you feel it's not right for you, then they probably feel you're not right for them either. It's okay. They are great people, and I'm still friends with most of them. I still partner with them and offer to collaborate on projects. There is no harm in making a mistake in your career. You can make lots of them and still be just fine."

> **Frankly, I want to do my job to the best of my ability, and then I want to live my life. I want to have fun, enjoy my family and dogs. I want to have a hobby again, which are things I haven't had much of in twenty years!"**

Another lesson Tina learned is that much of what motivated her earlier in her career changed over time. The constant need to strive and achieve fueled by the fear of not being successful took a back seat to other priorities. She ended up taking a job working at a firm that employed a number of her old friends. Together, they are managing a billion-dollar carve-out of another extremely large company. As Tina tells it, "Even though the work I'm doing now is probably the most difficult work I've ever done, it is so much easier because I'm working with people I know. It's like shorthand. We all know how each other works, which makes it easier to cope no matter how challenging the project. I consider myself very lucky to be doing what I'm doing and working with these people."

Tina admits there are trade-offs, but she doesn't mind. She's doing a job again that she did earlier in her career, and she's not making as much money as she once did. She's also not interested in climbing the corporate ladder anymore. "Frankly, I want to do my job to the best of my ability, and then I want to live my life. I want to have fun, enjoy my family and dogs. I want to have a hobby again, which are things I haven't had much of in twenty years! I used to decorate houses that my ex-husband would sell, and I realized that is something I actually love to do. I'm decorating again, for me this time, and I love fashion and entertaining. I'm learning that there are a lot of things I enjoy doing."

Tina used to feel guilty whenever she wanted to do something for herself. She couldn't explain why she felt that way, but now she's at a place in her life where she doesn't feel bad about following her bliss. "I always felt I needed to take care of other people first," she says. "I remember for years and years I would work holidays so my colleagues could take their kids out trick-or-treating or head out early for a family vacation. And because I worked primarily with men, I would cover for them and work later hours so they could coach their kids' sports teams. I was happy to do it. Then, when the planes hit the World Trade Center, we let everyone take the rest of the day off. I stayed behind with a skeleton crew that called all the employees working at off-site locations to make sure they were okay. As I was leaving work that day, I had a chill go through me that caused me think that maybe I needed a little support too. I was by myself in Dallas, and my family was back East. It was a scary time, and I felt vulnerable."

On the topic of feeling vulnerable, Tina also shared that she went a long time in her career before she felt any vulnerability or discrimination based on her gender. She has always had an outgoing personality and was frequently treated by colleagues as one of the guys. "As an individual sales contributor and later, as VP of sales, as long as I made my number, people didn't mess with me," Tina observes. "I've since come to see that many women don't get a fair shake because they don't present themselves like men do."

Tina is more motivated than ever to help women who feel discriminated against to be more visible in their careers, have more opportunities, and be treated fairly. "Let's face it, I wouldn't be in tech if the government hadn't told my first technology employer that they needed to hire more women and other minorities," she points out. "I'm now involved in women-focused organizations as a blogger and speaker on equality for women in technology. I think it's absurd that it's still an issue, and I am putting my energy into helping to turn that around."

More about Tina Gravel

Tina Gravel is an award-winning executive with more than twenty-five years of experience in the IT outsourcing, cloud, security, and SaaS industries. Tina is currently SVP Global Channels for Cyxtera—a technology company that exists to create a truly secure hybrid IT environment with interconnected site colocation and data center services (cyxtera.com).

Prior to Cyxtera, Tina was a Senior Vice President of Global Channels and Strategic Alliances for Cryptzone, a Cyxtera Business. Before joining Cryptzone, Tina held the role of General Manager and Vice President for Dimension Data's Cloud Services Business in the Americas. Tina also served as Vice President of Worldwide Sales and Marketing at Nirvanix, leading the company's sales, marketing, and indirect channel programs.

Tina was a member of the original management team at Terremark, a Verizon company, where she held several leadership roles more than fourteen years, including Vice President of Global Channels and Alliances, Managing Partner for the IT outsourcing (ITO) business, and Vice President of Terremark's Central Region Sales operations. Her guidance helped take the company from $400,000 in annual sales in 1999, to the acquisition by Verizon for $1.4 billion in 2010.

Tina also gained additional sales experience in senior positions at leading IT companies including NetGravity (now owned by Google), SAS, Sybase (now owned by SAP), and CSC. Tina has also worked as an independent consultant, helping start-up technology organizations increase their revenue, monetize their intellectual property assets, and obtain funding.

Tina has had published articles in many publications, serves on the Advisory Board for Channel Partners Magazine (now a Penton Company) and the Executive Board of the Illinois Technology Association.

Follow Tina on LinkedIn (Tina Gravel) and Twitter (tgravel). She can also be contacted at tgravel536@gmail.com.

CHAPTER 7 _____

A Conversation with Natalia Botti Schenkel

Channel Sales Director, Midwest at Fuze (fuze.com) and Women's Leadership Blogger and Technical Evangelist at Compute Style (computestyle.com)

_____

Creative Process

1. This is awesome
2. This is tricky
3. This is shit
4. I am shit
5. This might be okay
6. This is awesome

—Jess Levitz, graphic designer,
lettering artist, blogger, juneletters.com

First, a Few of My Thoughts

In this chapter you're going to get to know another highly creative woman, Natalia Botti Schenkel.

To cue up Natalia's chapter, I wanted to consider creativity, starting with the quote from Jess Levitz. I'm enamored with this quote, which sums up my creative process perfectly. Whether I'm creating a relationship, a career, a workshop, a book, a... life, this is my process. I start off confident, generally because I don't know what I don't know. Then, when I delve into whatever I'm creating, I see how hard it is or how much work I have to do. I question myself, beat myself up, work through it, and after a period of time, start to see it's not all bad. Eventually, I feel good about what I created.

How about you? How does your creative process work?

Think about it. You want to know how your creative process works, because you are a creator.

Yes, you are a very creative woman! Every moment of your life you're creating threads of experiences that, when combined together on the loom of life, create a unique (and may I add gorgeous) tapestry. The tapestry of you.

But this notion of being a creator—a creative person—is tricky for most. Part of the trickiness is our interpretation of what it means to be creative. If someone is good in music, dance, art, acting, or writing, it's common for people to say he or she is creative. If someone is not naturally predisposed to music, dance, art, acting, writing, or other obvious "creative" activities, he or she may be more likely to tell you they're not creative.

But they are. We all are.

Creativity is the expression of talent. And we all have talents, many of them, in fact.

Not sure what your talents are? Let your curiosity lead you. Curiosity and creativity go hand in hand.

Your curiosity most likely compelled you to pick up this book and start reading it. And why not? Ultimately, it's a book written just for you. It's a book about how you can be a woman working in the world of technology while creating a life that matters most to you—and more.

So what matters to you? It's okay if you can't readily put your finger on that right now. I assure you though, as you continue to read this book, certain stories will resonate with you.

Be curious about these stories, because they hold answers and important insights. I have found that being curious often leads to discovering what matters most to you, and in some pretty miraculous ways. I also found that when I stopped being curious and tended to think I had all the answers (a truly laughable notion), I was actually quite confused and certainly not focused on what mattered most to me at the time.

Let me give you an example. But first, here's the context.

Growing up, I was frequently told that I was a curious child. I remember when I was about four years old, my mother's older cousin, Dorothy, came over for a visit. She was sitting at the kitchen table, and my mother and aunt were fixing lunch. I came into the room and sat next to Dorothy. I couldn't take my eyes off of her. It was as if she was the only person in the room. I had never met her before, and I started asking her questions about anything I could think of through the lens of my life at the time. Where are your children? Why don't you have any children? Why do you work? What do you do at work? What's your favorite cookie? Apparently, the barrage of questions was impressive enough to cause Cousin Dorothy to bust out laughing, while exclaiming to my mother that her daughter was "something else." Over the eighty-six years that dear Cousin Dorothy was on the planet, she would tell this story over and over again. The story of this strangely curious little person, this mini investigative reporter, who was genuinely interested in getting to know her.

Fast-forward four decades. I had been a woman in business for quite some time and just left a high-level position working for a corporate training company to start my own organizational development practice. I also had several books in me fighting to come out and thought that I would begin to write one of these books as well. Over the years, people would tell me "you could write a book, you know so much." I thought I'd give it a whirl.

Whenever I sat down to write the book about what I knew to be true about creating strong organizations, I would inevitably get involved in other projects, and the idea of writing (and finishing) the book lost its luster. This pattern would repeat itself over and over again, and with different book ideas, across a span of fifteen years.

You see, in the process of thinking I knew so much, I lost my sense of discovery. I lost my curiosity and my capacity to create something that mattered to me.

Once I realized I truly knew little about anything, my four-year-old self re-emerged, and I started asking questions again. Which led to writing and publishing two books in two years. I love to ask questions, learn about people, places, and things, and then write about what I learn. For me, that's the best kind of book. Not a book just about my experiences and thoughts, but a book that brings together the experiences and thoughts of many.

This is one of the ways I create; this is my "art."

Now let's get back to you. You are in the process of creating a life that matters most to you, and matters to others as well. You have a story to tell, and one day maybe you'll let me tell your story. How exiting would that be!

While we're pondering exciting possibilities, let me tell you a little more about our chapter focus—Natalia Botti Schenkel. She is a helluva creator with a singularly spectacular story. And she has a generous spirit and genuine warmth that instantly draws you to her. You want to get to know this woman!

When Natalia learned about the possibility of being interviewed for this book, she tugged at my heartstrings when she told me "I would love the chance to assist your efforts and provide additional value if selected. Although my career in tech is new, I've had one heck of a learning curve in a very short time. I would consider it an honor to share my story with other women who might be new or struggling with the climate of this field."

And boy oh boy, she wasn't kidding. Just wait until you read what she has to share.

Though she didn't know it at the time, Natalia's big break in tech came when she took a back-office job at a telecom company. She quickly learned the business, advancing from performing cable serviceability checks to learning all she could about telecom carrier operations. Her initiative did not go unnoticed, and the owner of the company suggested a promotion into a sales position working in their call center. But Natalia thought she could contribute more to the company by working in their channel manager group as she felt it was a better fit for her talents. She asked him to give her a shot.

It just so happened that the company was struggling to keep one of their largest clients. The owner agreed to give Natalia a position in their channel manager group and assigned her to their largest account. The very account with which the company was having challenges. He told her "you're a cute girl, they'll love you to pieces." But Natalia remembered some advice a good friend told her—pretty isn't enough—and she took that advice seriously. She fully intended to contribute more than her looks.

"As I'm learning about the client's operation, I start to see where we could assist them," says Natalia. "I find holes and gaps in their portfolio and offer them ideas to help patch those holes and fill those gaps. I ended up taking the account from one that was losing money, to one that was bringing in more than $800,000 within two years."

And she learned a lot about herself.

> **In that moment after having that success with our channel group, I realized I can't make fun of myself anymore. When you allow yourself to feel a certain way or to project that out, it allows other people to project that back to you."**

After her success in developing the company's largest client, Natalia was surprised that she still was not taken seriously by her peers. She thought she had proved herself. Instead of getting angry, she took a hard look at her own behaviors and realized that her co-workers didn't take her seriously because she didn't take herself seriously.

"As an adult I was diagnosed with a severe form of dyslexia," says Natalia. "It was a revelation at the time because I had always struggled in school, and the diagnosis explained why I had trouble reciting numbers, reading, and pronouncing things correctly. As I was growing up, I used self-deprecating humor to mask my learning challenges. I felt stupid, but I knew I wasn't dumb. In that moment after having that success with our channel group, I realized I can't make fun of myself anymore. When you allow yourself to feel a certain way or to project that out, it allows other people to project that back to you."

" You don't have to wait for someone to tell you you're good enough, you're worthy, here's the door, come on in. It just doesn't work like that."

She also learned to appreciate and value her strengths, and she frequently tells other women to do the same. "If you're going to be in tech, you have to understand what you're good at. Some people are really good at storytelling and marketing, and that's the bubble I fit in. Other people are insanely good at operational procedures or have excellent technical abilities. When you know what your strengths are, you'll be led to the right path for you."

Natalia admits that when she first started in tech, she wasn't sure what her strengths were. She relied on other people to tell her what they thought she was good at doing. She then took that knowledge and did a SWOT analysis with herself, analyzing her strengths, weaknesses, opportunities for growth, and the threats that she thought were preventing her from moving forward. The exercise uncovered an uncomfortable truth.

"I had to get rid of my old story. I was stuck in it. Not everybody needed to know that I grew up extremely poor, didn't have food, or other details about my past. That's not who

I am. Who I am is an intelligent, helpful, creative, resourceful person. That's the story I wanted to build on."

Natalia wants all women to know that they are not products of their environments. They can make choices and create opportunities for themselves. "You don't have to wait for someone to tell you you're good enough, you're worthy, here's the door, come on in," Natalia says. "It just doesn't work like that. And if someone tells you that your idea is bad, that's when you go for it. Because that means there's an opportunity there that you see and someone else doesn't."

Natalia knows a few things about creating opportunities for herself. She got married right out of high school to a man from Lebanon. She was married for thirteen years, had two daughters, and had just miscarried twins. It was a low point in her life.

"I'm sitting there, and it dawns on me that I'm a horrible housewife. I make messes. Cleaning isn't my thing. I didn't know what to do with my life, but I knew I didn't want to stay home and make babies. I knew I was meant for something else."

One day Natalia caught herself humming a television jingle from a local college. She couldn't get it out of her head. "Davis College, it's all about where you're going," she sings. "And I thought, *Where am I going? What do I want to do? What does that look like?*"

 It's really easy to compare yourself to other people. It's really hard to just accept who you are for what you are and what you can be. And if you don't like where you are, you can always change it."

Natalia met with the college and told them about her struggles learning in a traditional school environment. She was scared and hadn't been in school for quite some time, but she liked what they told her and enrolled. With Davis she had her first educational experience where they invested in her as a human. They helped her identify ways she could learn more effectively in the areas of her greatest strengths. And she learned practical skills such as writing business letters and interviewing for a job. She completed her associate degree in business and marketing and then moved to Chicago to be closer to her father and to take advantage of a better job market.

"Davis College was a great start for me in continuing my education throughout my tech career," Natalia notes. "They helped me own my truth."

She continues, "It's really easy to compare yourself to other people. It's really hard to just accept who you are for what you are and what you can be. And if you don't like where you are, you can always change it. I've done that time and time again, and here I am. I have a wonderful life. I'm not living on welfare, and I don't have any of the problems I used to have. I have a whole new set of problems—great problems to have! I gained too much weight because I ate out too much. I've never been able to eat out too much. I love that!"

> **Now, whenever I'm faced with a situation that I think is sexist, I go by how it makes me feel. If it makes me feel uncomfortable, then it's wrong. I also set boundaries."**

Other challenges Natalia learned to navigate included some pretty serious instances of sexism. Certain occurrences were quite overt, while others were subtler. Natalia found that the latter were actually harder to deal with, because they made her question who she was and whether or not she was just making stuff up in her head. To gain clarity, she found one approach that worked particularly well for her.

"Now, whenever I'm faced with a situation that I think is sexist, I go by how it makes me feel. If it makes me feel uncomfortable, then it's wrong. I also set boundaries. I now realize that I'm not one of the guys. I'm never going to be one of the guys. When I walk in a room, I look a particular way, and it's not the same way they look. But I can be a woman they respect."

Natalia tells other women to have strategies they can readily use if faced with sexism at work. And don't wait for it to happen; be a person who behaves in a way that may actually prevent sexism from happening in the first place. For example, a small behavior such as saying your own name can tilt the interaction in your favor.

"I remember listening to a group of women doctors complain that they weren't getting respect from their patients. The issue they found was that in the process of helping their patients get comfortable, they weren't using their title of "Doctor" when they introduced themselves. That got me thinking, I'm not telling people my whole name—Natalia Botti Schenkel. Instead, I'm saying, 'Hi, I'm Nat,' now, when I introduce myself, I give my full name."

❝ I think a lot of times women don't want to speak up because they're fearful of saying something wrong or foolish. I mirror what the other guys around me do when they talk in the group. They're not afraid, and they don't seem to care as much as we do."

Another observation Natalia made is that men tend to talk mostly about movie quotes, sports, and money. So, she made a point to get more knowledgeable and comfortable talking about those topics. It helps her better relate not just to men but women as well.

Natalia also learned to find her voice and speak up. "You don't have to be the smartest person in the room or the loudest. But when you speak, people will listen if what you're saying is coming from a place of passion or conviction. And be okay hearing your own voice. I think a lot of times women don't want to speak up because they're fearful of saying something wrong or foolish. I mirror what the other guys around me do when they talk in the group. They're not afraid, and they don't seem to care as much as we do."

Natalia found value in reading Jessica Bennett's book *The Feminist Fight Club: An Office Survival Manual (for a Sexist Workplace)*. In the book, Bennett gives various scenarios and then asks, "What would Josh do?" For example, if Josh was part of a workgroup talking about a work problem and potential solutions, what would Josh do? Would Josh just sit there and say nothing? No. Josh would blurt out whatever he thought was a good idea or the most obvious solution. And Josh would get credit for that and his visibility in the company would be raised. It's all about putting yourself out there. And you don't have to have all the answers. You can simply say "Hey, here's an idea." The book is packed with great advice, and Natalia strongly recommends reading it.

> ❝ **And don't allow people to confuse your niceties for flirting. I'm a very nice person. I'm not a flirt. There's a big difference between the two."**

Natalia also has developed strategies for dealing with more overt forms of sexism. "I've been told some really horrendous, hardcore things. Along the way I figured if someone is going to make me feel uncomfortable by talking down to me or making a joke at my expense, I'm going to be quick-witted and come right back at them." Natalia will respond to the sexist behavior right away, even if other people are around. She found that it helps offenders understand that, one, they crossed a line; two, that she doesn't accept their behavior; and three, that now they are the butt of the joke, instead of her. She calls them out, and they stop their sexist behavior. She isn't malicious, though—she keeps her cool and keeps it light.

"And don't allow people to confuse your niceties for flirting," Natalia asserts. "I'm a very nice person. I'm not a flirt. There's a big difference between the two." Natalia has found that some men have a difficult time with making the distinction. "Making eye contact is not an open invitation."

Yet, experiencing challenges with interpersonal dynamics between men and women in the workplace is universal and not reserved just for the tech industry. Natalia has found that what is most important is to find the right people to do business with and make sure you've got the right culture fit. She's a big fan of being a woman in tech. "I think tech is so awesome because you can come from a place of nothing and turn it into something significant. I think it's one of the only industries that you can do that in."

And Natalia is realistic about who she is as a woman in tech. She knows that she's never going to be the person who will be known for her amazing programming abilities or for creating the next best application. She is perfectly okay with that reality. She also knows that she loves to learn, she loves technology, and she loves what you can do with the possibilities that technology brings. And, from her perspective, that's all she needs to keep propelling herself forward. It also led to her developing a side business in 2017.

"Since I was young, I've been heavily involved in style and fashion even though I grew up living on a pig farm," Natalia says. "I had an early interest in dressing a certain way and conveying a certain stature."

Natalia's interest in fashion led to her working as a retail sales associate for six years when she first started in business. Three of those years she worked for Talbots. While there, she began to understand style, image, and personal branding and how women dress in the workplace. She loved to work with the women who came into her store. She wanted to know what they did because they looked so polished, professional, and educated.

> **It used to be I received an award and I was happy, or I sold a really big deal and I was happy. Now what makes me happy is seeing what else I can do and doing things I didn't know I could."**

Many years later, she did virtual styling for some clients, and then a couple years ago colleagues from a professional women's group called "Cloud Girls" encouraged her to start a blog and Compute Style was born. "For the longest time I thought I could never do something like blogging. I have trouble getting words out! But the more I thought about it, I realized I had nothing to lose. I was spending more money on an outfit than I would hosting a blog. So, I went for it."

Compute Style focuses on empowerment and personal branding. To develop the content, Natalia had to take a step back and ask herself how she went from point A to point B in her career, and in such a short time. She felt that was the story she wanted to get out to other women. In a matter of months, the blog expanded to include an e-magazine, and Natalia has current plans to build her platforms further.

"I'm obsessed with analytics. I check my phone for stats to see how much traffic I'm driving, and when I change something up I can't wait to see how that affects the stats. It's like a giant social science experiment. Eventually, I'd love to get deeper into analytics to forecast fashion trends. That sounds like great stuff to me!"

Like a true creative spirit, Natalia is open to anything, attached to nothing. She's most passionate now about seeing what she can accomplish. "It used to be I received an award and I was happy, or I sold a really big deal and I was happy. Now what makes me happy is seeing what else I can do and doing things I didn't know I could. I still want the corner office. I still want all those perks. I just don't know where I want that office to be or what it will look like. And I don't think it will look the way I thought it would."

More about Natalia Botti Schenkel

Natalia (Botti) Schenkel is Channel Sales Director, Midwest at Fuze—a global cloud communications and collaboration software platform for business enterprises (fuze.com). Prior to joining Fuze, Natalia was a channel manager for INAP.

Natalia has seven plus years' experience creating and implementing business strategies for Fortune 500 and Fortune 1000 VARs and Technology Distributers. In 2017, she shifted her focus from traditional services to cloud and emerging technologies ensuring that both her partners and her company are advantaged by her abilities to deliver solutions that increase revenue generation, attract and maintain customers, and build corporate brands.

In addition to her successes in business development, Natalia continues to evolve her passion for next-gen technology centering on the support and personal branding of women business leaders through networking affiliations and, recently, through her creation of a women in tech style blog (computestyle.com).

Follow Natalia on LinkedIn (Natalia (Bolli) Schenkel); Twitter (compute_style); and Facebook (Compute Style). She can also be contacted at ITmeplease@gmail.com.

CHAPTER 8

A Conversation with Raquel Wiley

Senior Channel Marketing Manager, Channel Partner Program at TPx
  Communications (tpx.com)

Every one of us is a wonder. Every one of us has a story.
—Kristin Elaine Hunter, American writer

You must have control of the authorship of your own
destiny. The pen that writes your life story must be held
in your own hand.
—Dr. Irene C. Kassorla, psychologist, lecturer, author

First, a Few of My Thoughts

In addition to writing books and various corporate
communications, I create and teach human potential classes for
businesses and college continuing education programs. Earlier
in the day, before my scheduled interview with Raquel Wiley,
our focus for this chapter, I was putting the finishing touches on
one of my classes—a one-day workshop called *From Humor to
Health: Comedy and Healthy Living.* This particular workshop I
co-facilitate with comedian, actor, and radio personality, Dobie
Maxwell. Dobie is also a comedy instructor, comedy writer, and
nonfiction book author. He performs all over North America and
was featured on *The Late Late Show with Craig Ferguson.* He is a
master at what he does and an all-around great guy.

Dobie facilitates the morning part of the workshop, which focuses on how to get in touch with your funny side and share that with others. I teach the afternoon segment that introduces the health benefits of laughter and then shows participants some astoundingly simple tips and techniques to help chill out, lighten up, and laugh more.

I've taught my portion of this workshop at forward-thinking companies many times in the past. For me, it's hard to argue with the logic that when you have team members who know how (and when) to chill out, lighten up, and laugh more, they enjoy their days (and their work) more, and the company benefits. This type of "energy" work is catching on in more and more workplaces, and I couldn't be happier because I truly believe its time has come.

Now, back to Raquel. Later that day, when I phoned her for our interview, she asked if I could hold for just a moment while she turned off her music. I then came to find that she uses music, especially jazz and gospel, as a segue, assisting her as she flows from one activity or segment of her day to another. Music is part of Raquel's daily energy routine to set her atmosphere at work and more. It helps her to "tune in and get realigned" with her own personal energy. It helps her "get the noise out" of her oftentimes crazy, hectic day, allowing her to focus on the positive outcomes she seeks to accomplish.

That certainly made sense to me!

As does Raquel's other advice. From taking chances in life to holding herself accountable for your choices, Raquel has learned much and has a great desire to serve others by sharing her story.

"I believe in being transparent and in sharing some of my personal stories—good, bad, and neutral—that helped shaped me into the go-getter that I am today," relates Raquel. "And I have a real passion to serve and assist younger women on their journey. Another young lady may be challenged by the same things I experienced, and maybe she's worried about not making it or not having other options. It may be a little difficult at times, and the journey will be different, but I want her to know that if I could do it, she can do it, too."

Raquel is a big believer in taking chances and owning your life and the decisions you make. She authentically lives Irene Kassorla's quote, "You must have control of the authorship of your own destiny. The pen that writes your life story must be held in your own hand."

> **Having my daughter at a very early age made me who I am today. She made me grow up. She made me more determined than ever. Failing her was not an option."**

"I took a chance and made one of the biggest decisions in my life when my high school sweetheart and I got pregnant in my first year of college, and we got married and started a family," Raquel shares. "We could have made so many other decisions, but we took a chance."

Raquel continues, "That decision grounded me a lot faster than if I would not have had my daughter at the time. Life got serious for me very quickly. Having my daughter at a very early age made me who I am today. She made me grow up. She made me more determined than ever. Failing her was not an option."

Taking that chance also ultimately led to Raquel having the career she has today, though there were a few twists and turns along the way. Raquel opted to forgo her bachelor's degree studies and pursue a two-year computer programming certification. It was right before the beginning of the dot-com era, and computers were booming. She wanted to make a choice that would provide career growth opportunities so she could take care of her family—as fast as possible. Upon receiving her credentials, she was determined to be debt free and pay off her college loans. She hadn't received an offer to work as a programmer and was feeling the pressure to get a job. That pressure led her to take an excellent-paying job with AT&T's customer service contact center team. Though she did well in her customer service role and was tapped to participate in the contact center's leadership program, she still had her eyes on a technology career. Two years later her opportunity came when she was presented (and accepted) an offer to work for IBM as an AS400 specialist working with California universities.

At AT&T Raquel learned the basics of being a business professional, how to be accountable and seek additional knowledge. At IBM, she learned that having variety and change in her work was important to her. "IBM helped me put things in place and start setting my mark to build a career and not just a job. I would have stayed with them, but the long daily commute kept me from my family, and another good opportunity presented itself to return to AT&T, though in a different capacity. With this new opportunity, I was able to work my way up through the ranks, over the ranks, and into a different functional area, and I eventually landed in technology marketing. I've been with TPx now for seven years, and I can tell you that no two days are the same, no two interactions are the same, no two scenarios are the same…and I love it."

> ❝ **Yet, wherever you find yourself in your career, I really do believe that you have to learn how to take some risks and be okay with the outcome, especially if it's not what you expected."**

While Raquel advises women to take chances, she also recognizes that some women will be hesitant, and for good reason. "I think it's easier for millennials to take chances because it's in their DNA, more so than for women in their forties, who tend to be more reserved," she notes. "For women closer to and in the fifty-plus age range, I think they experience more fear in taking chances. Sometimes when you take a chance, the outcome is not always going to be what you want, and there is usually some level of risk involved. Some women cannot afford to take chances financially, and others may find themselves working in a company culture that does not allow room for error. Yet, wherever you find yourself in your career, I really do believe that you have to learn how to take some risks and be okay with the outcome, especially if it's not what you expected."

To illustrate this point, Raquel shares a story about her daughter who was interested in a business venture. Her daughter was unsure if it would be successful and was afraid to take a chance. "I said to her 'What do you have to lose other than a couple thousand dollars if it doesn't work out? You can replace that in a little bit of time. And even if the business doesn't make it long-term, you will win as an individual because you learned what it's like to be a business owner responsible for starting and running a business. I think that's a mighty big win no matter how you look at it.'"

Raquel is also someone who has learned to live each day to the fullest and encourages other women to do the same. She was reminded of how precious life is a couple of years ago when her children lost their father in an automobile accident. "That tragedy brought clarity to me that we are not promised anything but this moment, and we need to make the most of it. I know it sounds like a cliché, but you have to remind yourself that today is a brand-new beginning to be grateful for and that others are not as lucky—this might be their last day and some may not even wake up."

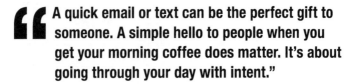

A quick email or text can be the perfect gift to someone. A simple hello to people when you get your morning coffee does matter. It's about going through your day with intent."

Another daily action worth considering is that Raquel wakes up each morning with the thought or expectation that something great is going to happen that day. Whether it happens to her or someone else, it really doesn't matter, she feels the same way. She also recognizes the connection between giving to others and feeling good herself. "I think women are natural givers. You give and give until you can't give any more. But why do you give? You give because someone is in need. You give because you find joy in giving, in making someone else's day. A quick email or text can be the perfect gift to someone. A simple hello to people when you get your morning coffee does matter. It's about going through your day with intent."

If you're getting the sense that Raquel is connected to her faith, you'd be right. However, that wasn't always the case. Though no one knew what she was going through at the time, she admits to losing herself in her twenties. When she ended her marriage at age twenty-six, she had to take a step back. She felt she had lost her identity and purpose. Although her work life was going well and she was financially secure, she felt an emptiness, as if something was missing.

"I found a faith-based community that felt comfortable to me," remembers Raquel. "And I did a lot of reading around sisterhood and the struggles of other women at the time, specifically books by Maya Angelou and Susan Billy. It helped."

When you're feeling low, Raquel recommends that you seek out and spend time with people who lift you up. For her, it was her grandmother and other elders who lived 1,700 miles away in Texas. "At the time, I felt like I failed my family," she recollects. "My kids were not happy having a mom and dad separated, and my friends couldn't understand why I needed to step away from the marriage. It was a very emotional time, and I felt a little lost."

> **I used to think I was the bomb-dot-com at the time, but I wasn't. I had to recognize that there were some things about myself that were not that hot."**

"I found that my grandmother and her generation had the 'secret sauce' to balance it all out. I didn't need another textbook. I didn't need another professional conference. What I did need was some good, old-school advice on how to do this thing called life. I was able to leverage the advice given, and it felt good to be a student in a different setting."

Between having a faith-based community and tapping into the wisdom of her grandmother, Raquel was able to take a deeper and more honest look at herself. "I used to think I was the bomb-dot-com at the time, but I wasn't. I had to recognize that there were some things about myself that were not that hot. I took ownership of the role I played in my marriage ending and challenged myself to be better."

> **We can be so focused on that next professional opportunity or promotion that our personal lives suffer without us even realizing it."**

The other factor Raquel found helpful on her path to self-awareness and personal growth was finding an "accountability partner." She describes an accountability partner as a life coach, a psychiatrist, a good friend—anyone who gives you permission to share your life goals and objectives with them and who genuinely wants to see you succeed. They hold you accountable by helping you keep it real.

"For me, it was a friend," Raquel says. "We didn't talk every day, but we had known each other for a long time. She was honest with me. She was the type of person that if you didn't want a real answer to something, don't ask her. She might bruise your feelings, but you knew she loved you. When she saw me doing something or heard me saying something that was not aligned with what I wanted to achieve, she'd call me out on it."

A final piece of advice that Raquel offers other women is an urgent reminder to never stop efforts to find the right balance between the personal and professional aspects of life. "You may be soaring professionally, but if once you get home behind closed doors you find yourself without any friends or someone to call in the middle of the night if you need a shoulder to cry on or a partner you can confide in, sooner or later you will feel lost. We can be so focused on that next professional opportunity or promotion that our personal lives suffer without us even realizing it."

Raquel admits that when she was looking for more balance in her life, she had to dig deep. She pushed herself to try new things to ultimately figure out who she wanted to be versus who she had become. She knew there was a gap between the two that needed to be addressed. "I had to ask myself, *What does Raquel Wiley look and act like when she's at the top of her A game? What are her characteristics?*

What does she like to do? I realized that I formed opinions and had interests based on what other people liked or didn't like. It's funny, but when someone asked me if I liked brussels sprouts, I would say 'no', though I never even tried them. So, I tried them, and guess what? I actually liked brussels sprouts! I really had to re-examine all my beliefs, for both the big and little things. When I focused on what felt good to me and not on what others told me would be good for me or what I should do, I began to get my life back in balance."

And, in the process, she found her true self.

More about Raquel Wiley

Raquel Wiley, a 20-year veteran of the telecom industry and channel marketing professional, is Senior Channel Marketing Manager for TPx Communications—a privately held provider of managed services including unified communications, managed IT services, connectivity cloud, and business continuity services (tpx.com). Raquel is responsible for the strategic planning and management of the TPx Channel Partner program, which drives nearly half of the company's revenue. She develops and executes a broad range of strategies and initiatives in support of indirect sales channel recruitment, enablement, and performance.

Raquel has been commended by channel partners for her exceptional collaboration and client interfacing abilities, as well as her planning, support, and process-development talents. Prior to joining TPx, Raquel was Associate Director of Business Marketing for AT&T where she provided end-to-end marketing management for the West Region small and medium business (SMB) sales organization.

After starting her telecom career in 1991, Raquel built her industry expertise with a steady progression of service, sales, and marketing leadership roles. Now a widely recognized leader in the telecom channel, Raquel gives back to the industry by serving as a member of the Board of Directors for Alliance of Channel Women, a not-for-profit organization dedicated to accelerating the careers of female leaders in the technology channel (allianceofchannelwomen.org).

Follow Raquel on LinkedIn (Raquel Wiley) and Twitter (RaquelWiley1020). She can also be contacted at raquelwiley@sbcglobal.net.

CHAPTER 9

A Conversation with Jess Bryar

Global Account Manager at Masergy Communications (masergy.com)

"Don't be afraid of your fears. They're not there to scare
you. They're there to let you know that something is
worth it."
—C. JoyBell C., author, philosophical essayist

Even to me the issue of "stay small, sweet, quiet, and
modest" sounds like an outdated problem, but the truth
is that women still run into those demands whenever we
find and use our voices."
—Brené Brown, author, excerpted from *Daring Greatly:
How the Courage to Be Vulnerable Transforms the Way
We Live, Love, Parent, and Lead*

First, a Few of My Thoughts

Within thirty seconds of meeting Jess Bryar, I just knew that this
was a woman who had found her voice in business and knew
exactly how to use it.

I was intrigued.

And absolutely amazed. Because once she began to tell her
story, she shared that she was able to find her voice in only a few
years after starting her career. That doesn't make her struggle any
less valid, mind you, it's just that such a quick transformation, in
my experience, is virtually unheard of! Who is this superwoman?
And how did she pull off such a daring feat?

You will have to wait just a moment for the answers to these most provocative questions, unless you fast-forward past this section. But first, please indulge me a minute more before you dig in.

A large part of Jess's story is around her transformation from fear to finding her voice and being fearless. My similar transformation took much longer than Jess's, and I experienced my fair share of peaks and valleys along the way. There were times when my voice rang clear, and then there were lapses when fear sunk its pointy little teeth into my tender psyche and wouldn't let go.

Fear has a way of doing that. Introducing self-doubt is its favorite go-to-market strategy. Let's look at fear in the business world today and consider a few ways you can put it in its rightful place.

The business side of fear is pretty straightforward. In the world of business, fear equals risk. Take a couple of introductory business classes and you'll learn pretty darn quickly that the best way to manage risk is with knowledge, experience, laws, professional guidance, assessments, education, systems, and processes, among various other nifty business tools. You'll also learn that while you can mitigate risk you can't get rid of it entirely. You have to learn to live with a bit of risk; you have to learn to live with a bit of fear.

One of the reasons I included the quote from C. Joybell C. is because I like it. I also have had some success putting her quote into action. Fear really is there to let you know that something is worth it. For me, it has been quite the motivator.

For years, I was afraid to write my own book. I ghostwrote for nearly fifty different executives over the years and had some of my own works published as well. I started writing a dozen different books at one time or another, but, although I hate to admit it, I was fearful of having my thoughts and passions rejected. Finally, I overcame my fear of rejection and published my first book on February 22, 2018. What made it worthwhile for me was the combination of relief (it's surprisingly like giving birth) and joy that it gave me. The joy came from the positive expectation that if one person took away something, *any*thing from what I wrote, I achieved my goal. If everyone else rejected what I had to say, that was okay by me, because to that one person I was of use.

I have also come to learn that feeling fearful for too long (again, the initial jolt can be helpful), is a colossal waste of time. Therefore, in the spirit of saving you some precious time, here are some quick, practical tips to consider adding to your "being fearless" toolkit.

First, before you let your fears get the best of you, take the time to examine them. A long time ago, I came across an acronym for FEAR—False Evidence Appearing Real. Usually, when you examine and get underneath a fear, you find that what you thought was real was simply in your head. You had no tangible *real* evidence that you had something of which to be afraid.

And, even if you do have evidence that what you fear will come to fruition, ask yourself "Is this a life or death situation?" Chances are, it's not. If your fear manifests, you will live another day. If it is a life or death situation, then let your fear motivate you to get the heck out and/or seek assistance pronto!

Another tip that's worked for me is to complete this statement, "If I weren't afraid, I would…" (insert what you would do). Remarkably, the very thing you would do if you weren't feeling that fear is exactly what you can do to overcome the fear. Crazy, right?! Try it.

Recently, I activated this strategy when I made the decision to leave a high-paying senior executive position to write books, create and facilitate emotional intelligence leadership workshops, and start a nonprofit that provides self-empowerment programs to women without resources or access. At the time, I was afraid that I was not using my talents to serve others. When I filled in the blank on the statement "If I weren't afraid, I would…" the answer was clear, and I began transitioning to my new career as author, trainer, and nonprofit co-founder.

What is your answer? What would you do if you weren't afraid? Let's see how Jess moved through her fear and into her own as a businesswoman.

"I was working in corporate finance and absolutely hated it, being tied to a desk and looking at Excel spreadsheets all day," explains Jess. "I was miserable."

Like many women, Jess went to college and selected a degree major not because she had a deep interest in the subject matter per se, but because what she really wanted to do instead was deemed to be an unsuitable career choice. "I was really good at photography, absolutely passionate about it," she reflects. "But my mom sat me down one day and said, 'you're never going to be successful as a photographer, there are too many in the world, pick something else.'"

Jess convinced herself that she was good in accounting because that was Mom-approved, and her brother had received his degree in it. When she graduated, she quickly landed a job in corporate finance and international business. Then one day she found out her company was filing for bankruptcy. It was the perfect opportunity to get another job. What she ended up getting instead was something quite unexpected.

"I'm interviewing with this accounting company and telling them how much I love numbers and how excited I get when everything balances," muses Jess. "They literally laughed at me and said, 'you're not an accountant.'"

Jess was floored. The company executives went on to tell her about an IT company they owned and asked what she thought about taking a job in technology sales. From what she knew about sales, she was not inclined and told them so. "I was young and unfamiliar with what sales entailed. I knew that most positions were commission-based and had heard horror stories from other people. I reacted pretty strongly to their suggestion. I said 'absolutely not, I'm not a used car salesman, it's unethical. I have to believe in the product if I'm going to sell it.'"

Jess couldn't afford to be unemployed though. Financially, she was on her own and needed to take care of herself, including paying down her student loans. She decided to take the job and crushed it. "Taking that job was the best mistake I ever made, because it led me to the position I have today. But those first years were tough."

> **There are plenty of employment opportunities out there where you don't have to be in a submissive role. You have to value yourself and your abilities."**

Jess experienced overt acts of chauvinism and was told that her job was to "wear a skirt and look pretty." She would open doors for new business, but once those customer relationships were won, she needed to turn many of them over to others. She was not allowed to run meetings and work certain solutions on the accounts she secured.

On the upside, during her first year with the company, she quickly built a reputation for being trustworthy and finding affordable solutions for customers that others had not previously suggested. "There were companies that my employer could not crack," Jess remembers. "But they started doing business with us because I was honest and gave good information that saved them considerable money."

Jess's work with small accounts, many of which were nonprofits, schools, small businesses, or accounts others did not want to work, paid off. She was the only one in her company at the time to be promoted from inside to outside sales in under two years. As she tells it, her secret for success was a combination of her personality and fear.

"There was a relationship with a school that my company was trying to secure for three years until I came on board," she shares. "I ended up building a great relationship with the purchaser there because we bonded over water manatees!

Then, when she was looking for certain servers, I found an excellent company that sold certified refurbished units at a cost that was $400 less per server than what she had been researching. The client was ecstatic and ended up saving a lot of money which meant a great deal since her school had little funding."

"I worked hard at that company. The hours were long—ten hours a day with a two-and-a-half hour round-trip commute—and I was terrified every day of losing my job. I had to be overprepared at all times to defend myself and survive. Now that I look at it, even though it was the worst job I ever had, without it I would not be at the place I'm at now. I'm very grateful to have had that early experience."

> **As I look back at that time, I had so many worthy ideas, but I never opened my mouth. I was petrified that someone would shoot my ideas down or think I was dumb."**

Jess's advice to other women is to know your worth and speak up. "Having experienced sexual harassment in the workplace has helped me to be a more confident person. Though if I ever experience it again, I would find another job. It's just not worth the battle. There are plenty of employment opportunities out there where you don't have to be in a submissive role. You have to value yourself and your abilities."

"And you can't be afraid to express yourself and share your ideas," Jess adds. "As I look back at that time, I had so many worthy ideas, but I never opened my mouth. I was petrified that someone would shoot my ideas down or think I was dumb. And don't be afraid to ask questions. I used to be so fearful that if I asked a question or showed any vulnerability or lack of knowledge, it would hurt me."

Jess asks plenty of questions now. She believes it's one of the reasons she has held a seat at an executive table. "I'm very accustomed to having customers and colleagues come to me for advice, because I'm not afraid to ask questions. It's all part of the research I do daily to learn all I can about new technology products and solutions. I used to work for a company where I had more than two hundred vendors whispering in my ear every day about how they're the best. That experience taught me the value to ask even more questions and conduct additional research on my own so that my opinion is never influenced by others."

Jess admits that she's a completely different person from the fearful young woman she was six years ago. One of the keys to her transformation toward being fearless was to work on her stage presence and public speaking. She was quite fortunate to have worked with one individual in particular, Marie Hale, who gave her this advice: when you're speaking in front of a group, no one wants you to fail. Jess describes Marie as "brilliant" and highly recommends her company—@revenue (atrevenue.com).

"Marie told me that the audience really is rooting for me and that they want me to succeed. That made so much sense to me because when I'm an audience member listening to someone else, I feel that way, too. There's nothing as painful as a nervous speaker. You absolutely want that person to do her or his best."

Jess continues, "She taught me techniques to convey confidence such as to use open gestures, stand up with uncrossed arms and legs, and get the crowd to say 'yes' within the first minute of the presentation. I was lucky to have her at my side telling me what to do and not do."

Jess also received excellent advice from two sales coaches who told her to challenge superiors and customers when necessary. Jess regularly puts their advice into action. "There was a time when I was given an unrealistic sales quota. Rather than accept the quota and make excuses down the road, which is typical for many in sales, I went to my boss at the time and laid out my reasons for why I thought the quota was unrealistic."

> **If you believe you are given an unrealistic goal, it's your responsibility to let the right people know."**

Jess was given a quota of $1 million for a program that was still in its infancy with sales of only $200,000 the previous year. She asked her boss for the factors that went into developing the aggressive quota so that she could project monthly incremental growth and track her own personal sales goals. She respectfully challenged the quota and gave reasons why she felt it was unattainable. She was factual and nonemotional in her delivery, and it worked.

"If you believe you are given an unrealistic goal, it's your responsibility to let the right people know," notes Jess. "I've had others tell me 'That's above my pay-grade' or 'I'm not important or smart enough to speak up'. I tell them that if that's what they believe, then that's how management will view them. You have to speak up for yourself and offer alternative suggestions, because no one else will."

 Technology is moving at too fast a pace to be complacent. If you're working for a company that doesn't value or invest in your learning, you have to fight for your right to learn, or find another company."

Today, Jess is most passionate about the work she's doing and her pursuit to learn more, further improve her quality of life, and give back to others. "As a technology consultant, it's my job to have the answers. I love the fact that I can help my partners grow their businesses and, essentially, close business for them by connecting them to the companies that most need their solutions and products. I also love that others come to me when they have questions. It's so empowering and rewarding to me that I'm this knowledge-base that people seek and value."

"I'm now at the point that I am known by many to be the prominent cloud industry expert and leader. I feel it's important in my new position at Masergy to receive regular training and education. Without it, I would not be as effective for my company. People talk about how challenging it is to leave work to attend conferences and training workshops because of their demanding workload. I get it. I also know that it can be equally challenging to steal away ten to fifteen minutes to watch a tutorial on your laptop on the newest technology. But you have to do it. Technology is moving at too fast a pace to be complacent. If you're working for a company that doesn't value or invest in your learning, you have to fight for your right to learn, or find another company."

Another career essential for Jess is to have a certain quality of life. "In my twenties I wanted to make as much money as possible. Now, I see that money is great, yes, but it isn't worth it if you're unhappy. I enjoy working from home with a flexible schedule. That's important to me. In the event that I do get married and have children, the fact that I work at a company that values and allows me to work at home is a great incentive."

Finally, Jess is committed to giving back to the tech industry through her work as the philanthropy co-chair for Cloud Girls. "We just did a campaign for Girls Who Code. The response was overwhelming. We exceeded our goals because so many people—men and women—see great value in giving young women these opportunities."

"It's awesome to see how women are gaining control of their careers in tech, but we still have work to do. I believe technology and finance are the backbone to every organization and that tech sales is a great career choice from a compensation standpoint. If you can get into a good company and you work hard, you can be set for life, but only if you're in an environment that embraces and values you. Remember you have a voice. Use it!"

> **At the end of the event, I had someone come up to me and politely and candidly say, 'it's good that you spoke up and contributed, I imagine as a female it's hard to be taken seriously.'"**

Also, make a point to use your voice *all* of the time, because what you do and say over the course of your career really does matter. Jess was recently running an event and was the only woman in a room of more than ten men. She knew many of the gentlemen in attendance from her work with her previous employer. During the introductions, a few of them shared that their reason for being at the session was Jess—and the fact that when she offers them advice and guidance, they listen. "At the end of the event, I had someone come up to me and politely and candidly say, 'it's good that you spoke up and contributed, I imagine as a female it's hard to be taken seriously,'" she retells. "He by *no* means was being offensive, just stating the truth and he was actually giving me a compliment. It is hard to be a woman in tech at times, and I will tell you I *still* have clients and partners who make me go through hoops to earn their trust. But once I have it, it is nothing but smooth sailing."

More about Jess Bryar

Jess Bryar is Global Account Manager at Masergy Communications (masergy.com). In this capacity, she is responsible for assisting the global companies served by Masergy with their global connectivity, network security, and cloud communications.

Before joining Masergy In March of 2018, Jess held the position of Sales Director—Cloud Solutions, for Sandler Partners. Over the course of her tenure with Sandler, she contributed to the company's success in distributing connectivity and cloud services. Sandler Partners has been recognized by *Inc. 5000* magazine for eight straight years (2010-2017) as "One of America's Fastest Growing Private Companies."

Jess earned her bachelor of science degree and corporate finance international business certificate from Colorado State University and holds several industry certifications.

Jess has a great passion for technology, especially IT infrastructure, and in helping companies shift from maintaining their technology equipment in-house to hosting it in the cloud. She is a current member of Cloud Girls (cloudgirls. org) and serves as their Operations Chair. Cloud Girls is an open, vendor-neutral, not-for-profit community of female technology advocates dedicated to educating themselves and their stakeholders about the vast and dynamic cloud ecosystem.

Follow Jess on LinkedIn (Jessica Bryar). She can also be contacted at jess.bryar@gmail.com.

CHAPTER 10 _____

A Conversation with Lisa Rom

Technology Business Development and Marketing Consultant

_____

> I do not wish women to have power over men;
> but over themselves.
> —Mary Wollstonecraft, English writer, philosopher,
> and advocate of women's rights

> Ninety-nine percent of the most difficult problems at
> work have nothing to do with "What" and everything to
> do with "Who" and, usually, it has to do with someone
> demonstrating a lack of emotional intelligence.
> —Cheryl O'Donoghue, author, businesswoman,
> emotional intelligence leadership advocate

First, a Few of My Thoughts

Lisa Rom was one of the first women I interviewed for this book. The #MeToo movement had just begun, and it was virtually impossible for two businesswomen in the United States to have a conversation without discussing the movement's extraordinary momentum. As we talked and Lisa shared her experiences, I couldn't help but reflect on my own as well. Both of us, working in male-dominated industries, have our share of stories of men in the workforce "crossing the line." The key, Lisa acknowledged, was staying above-board and professional, regardless of the prevalence of sexism in corporate culture over the years.

While gender imbalance in the tech industry can result in the discrimination and marginalization of women, it doesn't have to. When I listened to Lisa and her career strengths, one thing was clear: she did not rely on HR to come to her aid. Instead, she focused on her resilience and getting the job done. I believe most HR departments at established companies are staffed by talented hard-working professionals who have their hands full and, to some extent, their hands tied. While they are there to support women's rights and the rights of all employees in their workplace, they have to follow carefully constructed, lawyer-approved policies and guidelines. Many complain that the process takes too long and is not enough. And then there are the smaller companies that have few, if any, established HR practices.

To fill this gap, we need the continued efforts of all women to keep talking to each other, providing informal support and ideas for handling issues of workplace harassment and discrimination. Especially for those instances that lie in the gray area—situations that may be interpreted as not being "serious" enough to warrant attention or instances when you don't have the preponderance of evidence to make your case but you clearly have a concern.

Right before I started writing women-focused business books in mid-2016, I held a position overseeing human resources (and other departments) for a health care organization. I would frequently counsel executives and employees on a wide spectrum of sensitive topics, including those related to harassment and discrimination. It was always behind closed doors and guided by a rigorous human resources procedure. As is the case in most HR departments, the policies sought to protect all employees and the company from legal repercussions. Yet most policies did little to assist you in preventing these situations from occurring in the first place. They were mostly focused on what to do once you believed you were harassed or discriminated against.

As more of us speak up and share our personal and, often, painful stories, we are in a position to make it easier for others to share theirs as well. In doing so, we help address the gray area and fill the gap. And, while I'm an advocate for the HR department, I believe that few are equipped to handle the firehose of complaints from newly empowered women speaking their truth. Yet, this is perfectly okay, ladies, because there is no one HR department, company, or person who is going to "fix" workplace discrimination and harassment. It's our job, too. Let's add it to our to-do lists and get to it.

This chapter focuses on how one woman, Lisa Rom, has been able to thrive in a workplace environment dominated by men, in an era when sexism and harassment ran rampant. She tackled the gray area and not-so-gray area of workplace harassment, as well as other aspects of being a woman in technology. Lisa has an energy that is open, direct, and practical. I found her to be a no-nonsense soul. Her guidance in this chapter is forged by real-world experiences and a deep desire to assist you, me, and all of us on our journeys. Pay attention. This is another amazing chapter featuring a truly amazing woman.

Imagine you're a twenty-one-year-old woman, fresh out of college, who looks even more youthful than your young age suggests. You work in one of the most male-dominated businesses on the planet—the oil and gas industry in Texas. You're an auditor, so the men you work with naturally don't want you there, and they let you know it. The company HR department is exclusively focused on onboarding new employees and not protecting team members from sexual harassment (or any type of harassment for that matter). This is the environment in which Lisa Rom found herself firmly entrenched at the start of her career in the 1980s.

"The men I worked with intended to demoralize me as a woman, but it was probably one of the best experiences I could have had, because I had to learn how to not let that bother me," Lisa remembers. "I learned to play into their stories so I could get my work done. At the end of the day, they were harmless. But when they crossed the line, I figured out I could set them straight and they actually respected me more for it."

> **If they're being inappropriate, don't put any air in that sail. Be above it, and most men will get the point."**

Sometimes Lisa had to fly in company jets to the oil field or well. There was plenty of craziness swirling around her work environment, on the ground and in the air, from inappropriate joking to men openly seeking affairs. Lisa had to figure out how to work around the drama. It wasn't easy. Most of Lisa's clients faced little, if any, repercussions from the way they treated a woman in the workplace, especially a young one.

As an auditor, Lisa's job was to assess oil drilling and production operational processes and tell clients when something didn't meet the generally accepted standards. Typically, her clients would challenge her report when it was not favorable. Lisa says, "Here I am, telling them they have to change something they're doing, and they're telling me 'honey I've been here for thirty-five years, and I don't need you to tell me how to do my job.' I couldn't leave until they signed off on my report. I had to get used to working with men in a men's industry and not be intimidated by it."

One piece of advice Lisa has for women who find themselves working with men who make passes at them or make suggestive remarks is to diminish the effects of their comments. "If they're being inappropriate, don't put any air in that sail. Be above it, and most men will get the point," she notes. "When they see you're not fazed by their antics and you're not interested, they'll knock it off. If they wanted something more, they'll quickly realize that they're not going to get it from you. Sometimes the best defense is to minimize their words and actions by not making a big deal about it. But if their behavior is very aggressive or you're being bullied, you need a different strategy."

Later in her career, Lisa had a situation where she was bullied to the point that it was extremely difficult to work with the individual bullying her. While she was not sexually harassed, the person made it very clear to Lisa that he didn't want her there and told her so. For a number of months Lisa tried to make the business relationship work, but the lack of respect this person had for her was palpable. Though she provided documentation of his behavior to the company's HR department and asked for a transfer, nothing changed. Lisa decided it was time to move on. She knew she had done the best she could to remedy the situation, and she had to rely on herself to improve her experience. Sometimes it just works that way.

Later yet in her career, Lisa deployed a different strategy to combat harassment, and although others told her it was controversial, it worked. She recounts, "I had a situation where a male coworker from another department treated me really badly. No matter what I did, his disrespectful behavior continued. I was not in a high-level position at the time; I was part of a team that provided marketing support. When I spoke to my boss about it, she said I had to have a mediation session with HR. I knew that wasn't going to work, so I told her so. I also told her that I was not working with him anymore."

Lisa did not return her colleague's email. If he put a meeting on her calendar, she did not accept it. When her boss wondered how Lisa planned to continue with her strategy, Lisa asked her boss to trust her judgment in the matter and assured her it would all work out in the end. Lisa felt he really didn't need her to get his work done, and she didn't need him. Essentially, Lisa's strategy was another way to "take the wind out of his (harassment) sail".

"People said, 'you can't do that,' and I told them 'well, I'm an example of someone who just did,' and it was the smartest thing I could have done," says Lisa. "Because any interaction with him was not going to produce a better outcome, so why waste any more time obsessing about it? When he needs something done in marketing, he'll find another person to assist him, and I won't need to deal with his disrespectful behavior."

Lisa believes that we either have the power or we have the right to take our power, and women don't do the latter as often as men. "If you're competent in your job, and you know yourself well enough to know that something is important to your success, you have to take the necessary action and trust that the rest will work itself out."

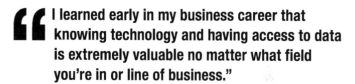 **I learned early in my business career that knowing technology and having access to data is extremely valuable no matter what field you're in or line of business."**

Another fascinating thing about Lisa was her path to becoming a woman in technology. After working as an auditor, her next career stop was in banking. She did project work in the accounting and finance department during a time where there were few software applications to support the work she needed to get done. This served as Lisa's entry point into the world of technology. As she recalls, "This was an era where corporations were building their own software; packaged software didn't exist. Non-technical businesspeople had to roll up their sleeves and become comfortable with the technology; you couldn't use the applications unless you understood how to put the data into the code."

Lisa was in charge of getting the reports to their chief accountant. She would travel across town to the IT department to get the reports pulled together, many of which involved highly complex customized analytics. "I was at the data center so much of the time that the guys decided it would be easier for them to show me how to code the reports myself. I learned early in my business career that knowing technology and having access to data is extremely valuable no matter what field you're in or line of business."

"It was then that I embraced technology, because it gave me the ability to be better at my job. I was also in the Silicon Valley when the dot-com era hit and the need was great for people with technology experience. As a mother of young children at the time, I found tech was the one industry where I could work part-time and stay in the workforce but still make a decent salary, and I never looked back. I was also really lucky to learn in an environment where everything in the industry was growing up with me."

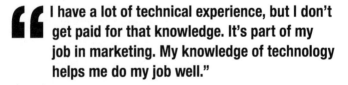

I have a lot of technical experience, but I don't get paid for that knowledge. It's part of my job in marketing. My knowledge of technology helps me do my job well."

Others in this book have advised women to broaden their understanding on the different jobs available in technology, and Lisa agrees that being a coder is not the only "real" job in tech. "I have a lot of technical experience, but I don't get paid for that knowledge. It's part of my job in marketing. My knowledge of technology helps me do my job well. Personally, I'd like to see more value given to people in nontechnical fields who have the technical expertise, because I know that is critical to career success."

A perfect example of applying technical expertise in a nontechnology field, per se, is the retail industry. Lisa recently supported an event associated with the National Retail Foundation in New York City. It is one of the biggest retail events in the world. The front-and-center topics were all related to the digital world, specifically, how to address the "Amazon Factor" and what companies can do to blend artificial intelligence with the retail experience. Lisa noted that just about everyone attending the conference, from the Nordstrom sales person to the owner/designer of a midsized regional boutique chain, is concerned about their place in a world where their top competitor is Amazon. Amazon, according to Forbes magazine, controls roughly 40 percent of the United States e-commerce market, offering the widest possible assortment of retail products at great prices.

Lisa sees opportunity in how we address the Amazon Factor. "As women in technology, let's unite around how to exploit technology to the best extent possible for the companies we represent and no matter what our jobs may be. Let's take advantage of budgets and corporate programs available that enable us to leverage technology and arm us with the information we need to make the greatest contributions at our companies."

Well-deployed technology, used in new and different ways, can allow businesses to leapfrog in their industry, product category, or new venture. And data is king in any industry. Although the majority of data scientists are men, Lisa believes women are uniquely poised to be highly successful in the world of big data and machine learning. It helps that we women are especially suited to make data-powered decisions and drawing insights from data. For example, there's a whole art about creating the right question; if you don't have the right question, you don't know what kind of data to be looking for. As women in business today, we can offer unique diversity in questioning and artful thinking that is so important in the generation of new ideas to advance our businesses.

> **Let's take advantage of budgets and corporate programs available that enable us to leverage technology and arm us with the information we need to make the greatest contributions at our companies."**

Lisa also believes that if more women were making more decisions and running more companies, it would be a dramatically different (and better) world, and she suggests that women look at ways to put their own financial contributions behind this thinking. For example, Lisa invests in SheEO, a Toronto-based nonprofit aimed at funding women entrepreneurs by changing the way businesses get funding (sheeo.world). Today, less than 4 percent of venture capital goes to women and less than 1 percent of corporate procurement goes to women-owned companies. Sadly, this is a widely reported statistic that has not improved in recent years despite the fact that 85 percent of all new products and services are created by women.

> **We give them a loan, we support their business growth, they pay back the money, and then the fund grows and grows. It really is transformative."**

SheEO was launched in 2015 by longtime entrepreneur, Vick Saunders, whose plan was to recruit groups of five hundred women who each donate $1,100 to a fund that makes below-market-interest loans of $100,000 to a set of companies founded and run by women. Only $100 of each donation pays for running the program, the rest goes directly to women-founded and -operated businesses. Lisa explains "My investment makes me an 'Activator,' which allows me to participate in the selection of businesses that receive SheEO funding. The product or service has to be transformational in terms of making the world a better place in which to thrive."

Lisa continues, "As an Activator I have access to other people who are activators. It's a very hands-on model, and we are really there to support these women entrepreneurs—not just in terms of the money we donate, but in being available to answer their questions. We are providing women with a support network as well as the funding. We give them a loan, we support their business growth, they pay back the money, and then the fund grows and grows. It really is transformative."

On the topic of transformation, Lisa has specific advice to women on how they can transform themselves, personally, in their careers. Her first recommendation is to know your company's products, be interested in them, and genuinely like them. "When I mentor people as they evaluate the next chapters in their lives, I suggest they take one to two hours each day to search the internet. Research your company's products and other like products offered by competitors. If you find some information on another topic, explore that as well. Don't feel guilty about taking that time on the company's clock, because you are advancing yourself and building a base of knowledge for you as well as your company. And don't worry too much if the sources you're reading are good or bad. You'll know the difference. You can tell."

> ❝ **When I mentor people as they evaluate the next chapters in their lives, I suggest they take one to two hours each day to search the internet."**

Lisa has also found that company salespeople, especially technical sales experts and product evangelists, are outstanding resources for product knowledge. Because they work closely with customers selling the product and, in many cases, helping customers overcome barriers that the product didn't address, they can offer an inside view that is particularly helpful. "Find a few solution technical salespeople in your company who are willing to be your subject matter experts when you need that kind of support," she notes. "I have found that they are very smart and honest, and they have the people skills as well, so they love to teach and train others. Find and align yourself with those people! They will help you be successful."

And find like-minded women. Lisa makes it a point to find women in her own company, as well as outside her company, who share common work perspectives and interests. It has helped her in her career, and it offers other perks. "The like-minded women I have met make the best friends sometimes. There is one woman, in particular, whom I absolutely adore. She's written a couple of books and recently went back to school to get her masters in cybersecurity. She did that all while she was working full time and raising two teenage boys as a single mom. She's a real role model for me, and we've become close friends. We make a point to get together once a month to talk about business—what we're doing and what we're hearing from others. There's no agenda, there's no competition. We just align with each other."

Let's put Lisa's words into action. Imagine how far we can get when we align with other women rather than compete. For therein lies our real power while paving the way for unlimited possibilities.

More about Lisa Rom

Lisa Rom is a sought-after industry consultant with expertise in IT solution and web security marketing and solution launches, service management, analytics, and ERP applications for both US and global markets. Her specialties are field and channel marketing; event management; product marketing and positioning; strategic partnerships and alliances; campaign development; and lead generation execution; among others.

Prior to establishing her consultancy practice, Lisa served as Global Strategic Alliances Marketing with Channel Impact @VMWare. The company markets innovative world-class enterprise software security solutions for both new and established markets, spanning multiple technologies including Cloud and SaaS (channel-impact.com).

Lisa also worked for Symantec as a senior manager, field and strategic channel marketing, where she provided diverse strategic and technical expertise in high-tech, healthcare, financial services, and SLED sectors, ranging from Fortune 100 to start-up companies. Other companies she has worked with over her impressive career in marketing management include: Ivanti, BMC Software, Inc., Charles Schwab, and Citibank.

Lisa received her bachelor's of accountancy, majoring in Accounting and Management Information Systems, from New Mexico State University. She is also a Certified Account Based Marketing Strategist—a designation she achieved in April 2016. Lisa is an active member of two trade organizations, Cloud Girls (cloudgirls.org) and Women in Technology (womenintechnology.org), and is in the process of writing a new book on high-tech marketing.

Follow Lisa on LinkedIn (Lisa Rom). She can also be contacted at lisatrom@yahoo.com.

CHAPTER 11 _____

A Conversation with Jennifer Pinson Herring

Sales Strategy and Business Operations Executive, RedBird Executive
  Group, LLC

_____

> What I have learned is that people become motivated
> when you guide them to the source of their own power
> and when you make heroes out of employees who
> personify what you want to see in the organization.
> — Anita Roddick, British businesswoman, human rights
> activist, environmental campaigner,
> founder of The Body Shop

First, a Few of My Thoughts

Jennifer Pinson Herring is an ESTP.

ESTP is an acronym used to describe one of the sixteen personality types created by Katharine Briggs and Isabel Myers. It stands for Extraverted, Sensing, Thinking, Perceiving.

This description is on Jennifer's LinkedIn profile. I smiled when I saw it, because it made so much sense. She leads people through change. And I have found that one of the best starting points for any change initiative—personal and organizational—is to start with having knowledge of yourself.

My smile broadened further when I also noticed that Jennifer listed her top talents based on Gallup's popular Top Five CliftonStrengths assessment—Futuristic, Responsibility, Significance, Relator, Maximizer. I have worked extensively with this assessment throughout my career and find it to be a useful tool to gain powerful self-knowledge and, perhaps even more compelling, to provide wonderful descriptions of you and how you operate that you can use to communicate more effectively with others and build stronger work relationships. Self-knowledge is even more powerful when you share it with others. And when a whole organization uses this strengths language and learns how to respect and work with each other's strengths and differences, well, in my opinion, it doesn't get much better than that. (As a side note, if you have not taken the Top Five CliftonStrengths assessment, go to www.gallupstrengthscenter.com or buy the book StrengthsFinder 2.0. They also have another assessment called CliftonStrengths 34 which is worth checking out as well.)

The third thing I noticed when I looked at Jennifer's profile was the recommendations she received from others. I found them to be quite telling as to her values and what makes her tick. One specific phrase that attracted me was the description of Jennifer as a "servant leader."

Servant leadership is both a leadership philosophy and set of leadership practices. Traditional leadership generally involves the accumulation and exercise of power by one at the top of the organizational chart. By comparison, the servant leader shares power, puts the needs of others first, and helps people develop and perform as highly as possible. Empowerment of all is a front-and-center goal.

I think it is time for more servant leaders. Although progress has been made, still embedded deep in our DNA is this notion that leaders are "bosses" who are catered to, flattered, fawned over, and adulated by others. They do not serve their employees.

That's not their job. This notion has to go. It simply doesn't hold water. And more and more workers aren't buying it either. It's okay to be a leader *and* serve others, especially those who report to you. It feels good to be of service to everyone with whom you work, not just your superiors.

With that in mind, let's get an inside view into how Jennifer accomplishes the extraordinary feat of being a servant leader and her journey to becoming the businesswoman she is today.

What Jennifer loves to do, both in her work at the office and in the community, is to lead people through change. It is deeply satisfying to her to help others get through circumstances in their lives and to see opportunities and possibilities that they had not known existed.

On the work front, her passion for leading people through change began to take shape early on in her career with Accenture. It was there that she was given the opportunity to build a team that had never existed before, which at the time was called "People Practices." In this new role, she was able to put into action her "Relator" and "Maximizer" talents (as identified when she took the CliftonStrengths assessment). Jennifer has a natural ability to relate to people on an individual basis, figure out what they are passionate about, and what they want to do professionally. In many respects the new department she created was like a career coaching practice. "I learned that I love having those types of coaching conversations," says Jennifer. "I feel such gratification when I watch people who have been part of my team move on to other roles greater in responsibility and scope."

As her career advanced, she took a position with Rackspace. The company was growing rapidly, and the need for leadership talent was great. While she directed the company's enterprise sales and service delivery team operations, she spent just as much time identifying future leaders to become team leads or managers in her own units, as well as others to lead groups outside her departments. "I was able to see very quickly their strengths and match them to the right role, giving them the opportunity to use their strengths and talents to their fullest potential," Jennifer remembers. "One of those individuals I mentored during this time became the director of a Google business, another became a senior leader for VMware, and another became a senior manager running an enterprise operations team. There have been many, and it has been deeply rewarding to me to see their successes."

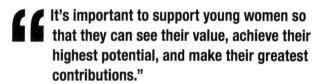 **It's important to support young women so that they can see their value, achieve their highest potential, and make their greatest contributions."**

Outside of work, Jennifer also has a strong desire to be a mentor and role model for young women. She serves as vice chair on the Board of Directors for Girls Inc., a San Antonio nonprofit that works to inspire all girls to be strong, smart, and bold. The organization equips girls to navigate gender, economic, and social barriers to grow up healthy, educated, and independent.

"My passion for the mission of Girls, Inc., stems from being raised by a single mother and being a single mother myself for nine years," Jennifer relates. "It's important to support young women so that they can see their value, achieve their highest potential, and make their greatest contributions. This type of support wasn't readily available to me growing up."

Upon graduation, Jennifer attended Stephens College in Columbia, Missouri. Stephens is an all-women's school, and although Jennifer only spent her first year there (she graduated from Texas Tech University), that experience prompted an epiphany for her. "I remember sitting in a classroom with all women talking about philosophy, religion, and politics," Jennifer reflects. "It was interesting and exciting, and I realized that I had a voice. I had something to contribute. That was not my experience in high school. It was at Stephens that I began to see that I could do something significant in my life. And that's exactly why I now share my time and experience with other young women who are also craving somebody to recognize the potential in them."

While it's ideal to have someone help you recognize your potential, Jennifer advocates the importance of gaining knowledge of yourself through your own efforts as well. She has found that personal assessments like Myers Briggs and CliftonStrengths can go a long way to help you discover who you are and how you can contribute at work and outside of work in fulfilling ways. The knowledge provided by these assessments also helps you understand why you operate the way you do.

"When I took the CliftonStrengths assessment, it indicated that one of my top talents was 'Futuristic.' I thought that sounded like me because I love strategy and looking forward. But with Futuristic as a strength you have to be careful because you can get too far ahead in your thinking about what something could be versus the reality of how it is. On the plus side though, I use my Futuristic strength when I share with my team a vision for the future and what something can be and then show them how we can get there."

> **But make sure that you have a plan or an endgame for every job you have. Know what you want to get out of that job."**

In addition to possessing self-knowledge, Jennifer has found it essential to have a plan for each job to help stay focused on your personal path. "Sometimes early in your career, you don't know what your personal path is. You're still in discovery mode. But make sure that you have a plan or an endgame for every job you have. Know what you want to get out of that job. Have a vision in your mind of what success looks like at that job for you, based on your needs and the needs of the business."

As someone who likes to lead people through change, Jennifer is happy she landed in technology. Like many of the women featured in this book, Jennifer came into the technology world through happenstance. However, what has kept her so engaged over her long career is the constant innovation and evolution of technology and the myriad changes that brings.

"Because technology is always changing you need to always look for new skill sets and for opportunities to broaden your knowledge because you have to adapt to change."

> **When you identify the different stakeholders, you begin to speak to them based on their role, and that helps you better understand how they're examining the decision."**

You also have to work smart. Being a woman in the tech space, Jennifer has found it highly beneficial to understand how company decisions are made, what the company financials are, how to build a diverse network, and how to cultivate resiliency.

When it comes to understanding how your company makes decisions, Jennifer recommends that you identify all the different stakeholders who will be part of a given decision—the actual decision-makers, the influencers, and the implementers. "When you identify the different stakeholders, you begin to speak to them based on their role, and that helps you better understand how they're examining the decision," she notes. "When you understand their roles and viewpoints, it benefits everybody—you and your clients. It benefits you because you understand how decisions are made in the company, and you can see more clearly the thinking behind each decision. It also puts you in a position where you can communicate that decision to your clients who may be impacted by it, helping to develop and strengthen client relationships further."

> **When I started my career, I was given the advice to take a financial course, and I did. I use that information every day."**

Another recommendation that Jennifer suggests is this: if you don't feel confident in your understanding of your company's financials, don't delay, and get the training you need. "When I started my career, I was given the advice to take a financial course, and I did. I use that information every day. Financial information plays a role in selling solutions to clients, explaining decisions to employees, and running the business. You have to understand financials and the role those financials play in your company."

On the topic of how to build a diverse network, Jennifer has found that though it's good to join industry or special groups and connect with others in person and virtually, it's not enough. You have to leverage those activities by taking an active role. "My advice is to get involved and be engaged with at least one group, even if you realize the group is not exactly for you," she shares. "You probably will make at least two to three new connections who will then be willing to connect you to other people. The networking piece is pretty big, because you never know when it's going to come back to you."

A final piece of advice Jennifer offers is on the importance of cultivating resiliency and getting back up after being knocked down or suffering disappointment, even when you feel that life is blasting you with a firehose. "In 2007, I left a ten-year career with Accenture, had a baby, moved to a different state, bought a house, got a divorce, and started a new job in a matter of twelve months. I didn't stop to think about all the things that were happening, because I was doing everything I could just to get through it. I knew I had to make it because I had a child and she was depending on me. I had to make money or we were going to eat ramen noodles longer than I intended. Man, I felt knocked down. But I got back up."

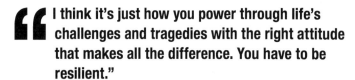 **I think it's just how you power through life's challenges and tragedies with the right attitude that makes all the difference. You have to be resilient."**

Another time when Jennifer's resilience was called into action in a life-altering way was in early 2017. It was on that day she received news of a company-wide layoff and was let go. It was a tough blow for her, because she loved her job and was personally invested in building the business and growing the company from 1,000 employees to more than 6,300. "I remember thinking to myself 'Oh my God, I can't believe this is happening,'" Jennifer says. "It's a year later, and I'm in such a better place personally and professionally. I feel so grateful and blessed. I mean, how awesome is that! You can't see the good things ahead when a change like this is happening to you. I think it's just how you power through life's challenges and tragedies with the right attitude that makes all the difference. You have to be resilient. You have to just move on."

Wise words from a master change agent with a fair share of change under her belt. Just the person you'd want to help show you the way.

More about Jennifer Pinson Herring

Jennifer Pinson Herring has twenty years of experience in the technology industry. Most recently she started her own growth strategy consulting business, RedBird Executive Group, LLC. Before that, Jennifer served as vice president of sales with 3Sixty Integrated and as director of strategic technology alliances and channel sales for San Antonio-based managed cloud company, Rackspace Hosting. During her nine-year career with Rackspace, she helped to drive revenue growth and market share to enterprise level customers globally through solution selling, strategic partner alliances, and go-to-market plans. She also spent ten years at Accenture during which she held the position of location operations manager in the company's Global Workplace Services division. In this capacity she was responsible for leading local Facilities and Services strategic business planning and contributing to global workplace planning.

Jennifer has a successful track record of identifying new revenue streams and expanding market reach. Her experience in business consulting and sales, servant leadership style, and "customer first" attitude are all contributing factors to her career success.

Jennifer is a member of Vistage, Social Venture Partners and Cloud Girls. She is also a member of Impact

San Antonio, Northside Chamber of Commerce, S.A.L.E. 4Kids, and Tech Bloc, and serves as vice chair on the board of directors at Girls Inc. San Antonio. Pinson Herring holds a bachelor of science degree from Texas Tech University and a general management certification from the University of Texas, Austin.

Follow Jennifer on LinkedIn (Jennifer Pinson) and Twitter (JenniferPinson1). She can also be contacted at jmspinson07@gmail.com.

CHAPTER 12 _____

A Conversation with Amy Bailey

Vice President of Marketing, Telarus (telarus.com)

_____

> You may believe that you are responsible for what you
> do, but not for what you think. The truth is that you are
> responsible for what you think, because it is only at this
> level that you can exercise choice. What you do comes
> from what you think.
> —Marianne Williamson, American spiritual teacher,
> author, lecturer

First, a Few of My Thoughts

Do you want to advance your career?

Take Amy Bailey's advice—think and act like a business owner.

But exactly how does one do that, you may ask? Amy's story will reveal a number of ways. More on that in just a moment.

When Amy started sharing her experiences with me, I connected with her right away. I know what it's like to be in a family business early in your career. Before we got married, my husband and I owned a retail video store and electronics repair center. My soon-to-be mother-in-law and two soon-to-be brothers-in-law were on the payroll as well. Some of my best business lessons came from that experience. At age twenty-three, I had a crash course in managing a tight budget and controlling expenses, while learning how to tune in to customer needs and demands in an oftentimes emotionally-charged environment. Working with family, especially in a busy seven-days-a-week retail operation, can have its challenges! But I also learned to put the business needs first while respecting the individual and to take emotions out of decision making.

To stand in the shoes of a business owner, you have to shift your mindset. And once you make that shift, you will never think about your job and how you do your job the same.

You'll also get some positive attention.

Employers love an employee who thinks like them and can demonstrate an understanding of what it's like to be responsible for running a business on all fronts. If you're looking for a way to differentiate yourself even further and make your mark in your company, this chapter will give you a healthy dose of insights and that little extra edge.

Amy was in high school when her father leveraged his telecom experience and founded a technology sales company, *CONNECTIONS* (callaccounting.com). *CONNECTIONS* specializes in call accounting solutions, and thirty years later the company is still going strong. For Amy, she grew up in the business and had a surface knowledge of the products they sold. While she was fascinated with all the different technologies, she didn't see herself having a career in tech after college.

Amy managed a retail department for Nordstrom and moved up to managing retail stores for Ann Taylor and Brooks Brothers. She enjoyed the work but not the commute. She was in her mid-twenties when she worked for Brooks Brothers in downtown Los Angeles. Her round-trip commute from Orange County was three hours each day. When the company opened a store close to her home, she put in for the store manager's job immediately. But she didn't get the position.

"I was devasted," says Amy. "My dad suggested I work for his company over the summer and if I didn't like it, I could go back and get a retail job around Christmas. I said 'okay, that works,' and I quit my job with Brooks Brothers."

During her first week on the job at *CONNECTIONS* she worked a major tradeshow for Nortel (now Avaya). Though she knew little about what was going on, she was hooked. "That tradeshow was a great entrance for me. I loved the technology. I loved the people. The energy was really cool. I remember thinking to myself *this could actually turn into something.*"

It did. Amy took the initiative to fully immerse herself in the business. It was 2004, and Voice over IP (VoIP) was catching fire as a hot new methodology and group of technologies for delivering voice communications and multimedia sessions over Internet Protocol (IP) networks, such as the internet. It was easy for someone new to become an expert fairly quickly because everything was changing so fast. In a short period of time, Amy became a star sales person for her father's company.

> **My family is from Iowa and there's something about that Midwest stock. You just roll up your sleeves and do what needs to be done."**

In the years that followed, Amy built a strong network with many of the people who owned the technologies she was selling. One group of gentlemen, who owned VXTracker (a web-based call accounting system), told her they were looking to sell their company. Amy mentioned this to some folks she knew well from another company she thought would be a good buyer for the VXTracker technology. She helped introduce the two companies, and before long, a deal was made. In the process, Amy got her first taste in channel management. Shortly after she helped broker the deal, the channel manager working with VXTracker left, opening an opportunity for Amy.

Amy retells what happened next. "The new company CEO who bought VXTracker went to my dad and said 'I really need to hire Amy because she knows the product better than anybody else. She can still be your channel manager, but I need her to help us bring VXTracker out to more clients.'"

Amy's father gave his full support and encouraged her to take the offer. He knew that becoming a channel manager for the VXTracker system would be an incredible career move for her. Though Amy left the family business to work for the manufacturer, she was still able to protect her parents' interest. It was a true win/win situation.

As a channel manager, Amy was part of a team that developed VXTracker into a suite of products. She especially enjoyed training new customers on how to use the application because it kept her deeply entrenched in the technology. Over time, they added more VX products and the software was relabeled VXSuite.

Her passion for VXSuite was infectious. Her head and heart were definitely in the game and she felt a strong sense of responsibility for contributing to the success of the products.

Her sincere enthusiasm and willingness to do "whatever it takes" led to her taking on marketing for VXSuite, in addition to being the channel manager. Over time, her success in marketing, which helped contribute to the remarkable growth of the VXSuite, resulted in an offer (which she accepted) to lead marketing for the company full time.

Event coordination and oversight accounted for a large part of Amy's work week. "In addition to all the events we regularly participated in, we decided to take on the crazy idea of hosting our own annual user and partner conference," she notes. "We rented out a venue at Lake Las Vegas, brought in fifty partner organizations, and had a channel partner conference all about VXSuite. It was a blast." It also helped to raise the company's profile in the industry.

Within two years the company was acquired again. This time by Telarus. "Telarus is a master agent, and master agents don't typically own technology products," observes Amy. "Yet they saw a lot of potential. Not only did we have a great group of partners selling the VXSuite, we had an amazing leadership team, and the technology was really great."

Three years later and Amy is still enjoying a fruitful career with Telarus as their vice president of marketing. She attributes most of her career success to the values she learned while working in her family's business. She recommends that women interested in advancing their careers can do so by developing a business-owner mindset.

Amy saw her parents lead by example. A business owner is always willing to do whatever it takes to get the job done.

You delegate when possible and let people do their work, but when something needs to get done, and there's no one to do it, no task is too small for a business owner. This is Amy's approach to her work today, just as it was when she held her first jobs in retail. "You have to be resourceful. When I managed a Brooks Brothers store and I saw the windows needed to be cleaned or the carpets vacuumed, I took care of it. If a shipment of clothes arrived, I signed for it, unpacked the boxes, steamed the merchandise out, and got it onto the floor. If someone ordered something to be mailed, I put it in the box and figured out the postage. Sure, I had a team, but we all took responsibility for getting the work done. My family is from Iowa and there's something about that Midwest stock. You just roll up your sleeves and do what needs to be done."

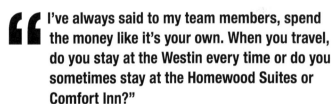 I've always said to my team members, spend the money like it's your own. When you travel, do you stay at the Westin every time or do you sometimes stay at the Homewood Suites or Comfort Inn?"

Another value Amy recommends is to be bottom-line focused. That means you carefully evaluate expenses, and you look for ways to do things more cost effectively without compromising quality. "I'm very frugal. When you have a family business, all the money you spend is your money. We didn't take our clients out for super expensive dinners, because that's not what we would do in our regular life. I see a lot of extravagance in the channel where people are buying the attention of partners. I understand that at times that can be necessary, but some of the extravagance is wasteful and not practical."

"I've always said to my team members, spend the money like it's your own. When you travel, do you stay at the Westin every time or do you sometimes stay at the Homewood Suites or Comfort Inn? Figure out what's wise. Make sure you spend the company's money in the right way."

Amy also reminds women to treat your clients like gold, because they are the lifeblood of the business. The more satisfied customers you have, the more success you and your business will have. She also makes it a habit to deliver more than expected. She believes when you give first and give more than expected, you'll get more in return. "I really work hard to get in the mind of my clients who are telecom agents and resellers. I'm always asking and thinking about what they need, how we market to them, and how we can create services for them that make their lives easier."

> **You don't cut corners. You do it right the first time and put your best effort forward so you don't have to do it over and you're not embarrassed by the quality of work you turned in."**

Amy regularly attends events and talks with her clients. She listens to what they say and gives them the additional attention they need. "The agents are doing so much. Their to-do lists are long, and many of them really need marketing support. I'll assist them with their website, flyers, business cards, and PowerPoint presentations. I'll give them education on social media and how to capitalize on LinkedIn and Facebook. It's an incredible amount of work, and it can be challenging, but it's important to take care of them."

Over the years people have commented on Amy's approach to work and how she takes responsibility for her employer's business as if it were her own. "They tell me I'm such a 'go-getter,'" she shares. "But I don't see it that way. I tell them that if you want to keep your job and move up in the world, that's what you do. You don't cut corners. You do it right the first time and put your best effort forward so you don't have to do it over and you're not embarrassed by the quality of work you turned in."

And you continuously work to improve. Just like a growing business needs to improve and get better, you, as an employee, must have the same goal. "For many of us in tech, there is not a formal education plan. You have to go out there, scour the internet, go to classes, and talk to people to figure out the technology. And you have to have a strong will. You have to know where you want to go and what you want to do."

> **You have to be able to recognize what you're good at and partner with others who do things better than you."**

Something Amy found beneficial was to take the time to do the inner work to understand what she's good at and what she's not. She personally does not like conflict, so negotiating is not her strong suit. What she learned was that she didn't have to become good at negotiating, she just had to find someone who was.

"You're not going to be good at everything. When it comes to negotiation, I go to Paula McKinnon in our supplier management group. She's awesome and can negotiate the hell out of a contract. You have to be able to recognize what you're good at and partner with others who do things better than you."

Amy also suggests that learning how to communicate in writing and how to read common financial reports will help you become invaluable to your employer. "It doesn't matter if you went to school to learn how to write. Just start a blog or write a LinkedIn post. Just put your thoughts out there. And if you didn't take a financial management class in college, just go to your CFO or someone else who can help you understand a profit-and-loss statement."

The last point Amy relates is that while your work life is important, make sure you keep things in perspective. This means taking the time to focus on your personal life as well. "Right when my career with Telarus was taking off, two of my family members experienced serious health issues and I wanted to be there for them to help with their treatments and doctor's appointments. Professional challenges are much easier to tackle. You figure them out and move on. But personal challenges are not always that easy."

I'm on a lot of flights and when the flight attendant says put your oxygen mask on before you help others, you do it, right? Because if you don't, you're useless—to others and yourself."

To help her tackle challenges in her personal life, Amy takes care of herself. Every morning at five, she goes to boot camp for an hour. "Boot camp is my sanctuary," she shares. "There was a time when I couldn't go for four days and one of my employees asked, 'What's different about you? You don't have the energy you usually have.' I knew I had to get back to class. It grounds me. It's four percent of my day and it's *my* four percent."

"I'm on a lot of flights and when the flight attendant says put your oxygen mask on before you help others, you do it, right? Because if you don't, you're useless—to others and yourself."

Spoken like a true business owner. And a very wise woman.

More about Amy Bailey

Amy Bailey is vice president of marketing for Telarus, the largest privately held technology services distributor (master agent) in the United States (telarus.com). The company's dynamic agent-partner community sources unified communications, contact center, cybersecurity, data, voice, cloud, and managed services through a robust portfolio of 180 leading service providers.

In her role overseeing the marketing operation at Telarus, Amy is responsible for crafting the Telarus message to partners and suppliers and works closely with them to provide content, enabling them to market successfully to their customers both via to-channel and through-channel marketing automation. Her team is responsible for branding, messaging, communications strategy, product launch communications, web, social media, public relations, customer and partner loyalty, creative services, internal communications, and major events, including the company's annual Telarus Partner Summit, more than thirty-five yearly Telarus Innovation Conference events, and the Telarus President's Club sales incentive trip.

Before joining Telarus in 2015, Amy served as vice president of marketing for LVM, Inc, owner of VXSuite where she worked closely with the President and CEO to create and execute the company's branding strategy for its VXSuite product line, including the development of all marketing communications content. She was with VXSuite for more than six years. Before that, she worked as a sales representative for *CONNECTIONS*, Telecom Marketing, a position she enjoyed for eight years.

Amy is also an active member of the Alliance of Channel Women and has held leadership positions with the organization since 2016. She is currently serving as their sponsorship chair and board member. Alliance of Channel Women is an organization focused on collaboration, networking, and mentorship for women in revenue generating roles in telecommunications and IT (allianceofchannelwomen.org).

Amy graduated with a bachelor of arts degree in speech communication and liberal studies from San Diego State University. While there, she was involved in the university's student government and served as the Associated Students President. She was also a member of the Alpha Chi Omega sorority.

Amy enjoys being outdoors and spending time with family. She is an avid hiker and early morning boot camper. She also loves to knit—especially while on long flights.

Follow Amy on LinkedIn (Amy Bailey) and Twitter (amyknitter and Telarus). She can also be contacted at Abailey@telarus.com.

CHAPTER 13 _____

A Conversation with Humanity

_____

> Superstition is foolish, childish, primitive, and irrational—
> But how much does it cost you to knock on wood?
> —Judith Viorst, American writer, newspaper journalist,
> and psychoanalysis researcher

First, a Few of My Thoughts

There is no rational reason for not having a Chapter 13 in this business book.

None.

And yet I'm compelled to follow the guidance of the planet's largest manufacturer of vertical transportation systems—Otis Elevators—and the reported 85 percent of building owners worldwide who install Otis Elevators each year without a 13th floor listed on their elevator numbering.

Call me a triskaidekaphobic. Just don't call me on Friday the 13th!

CHAPTER 14 _____

A Conversation with Laura Romero

Director, Global Partners and Programs at Plex Systems, Inc. (plex.com)

_____

Whether they stem from business or personal situations,
our relationships are what support us, connect us, and
allow us to progress in all aspects of our lives.
Building fruitful and lasting relationships starts with
abandoning the conventional "me"-based thoughts that
are so prevalent in the business world and so easy to slip
into in our personal lives.

—Michelle Tillis Lederman, business author (*The
11 Laws of Likability*, *Heroes Get Hired*, and *Nail the
Interview—Land the Job*), named one of Forbes's Top 25
Networking Experts

First, a Few of My Thoughts

One of the greatest joys for me in writing this particular book was
that it allowed me to get to know each of the women who are
featured in this first section. Talk about a dream team.

While I had not known any one of these incredibly giving,
thoughtful, and talented women prior to writing the book, I can
honestly say I'm a better woman for knowing them now. I'm also
honored that they trusted me to help tell their story so that you,
my wonderful reader, could get to know them too.

I hope you're also beginning to feel the collective energy
of those who participated in this book, including me. We all

care about your journey as a woman working in technology. Together, we are galvanized by our desire to serve and support you. We are on your team.

Are you ready to meet another member of Team You?

Her name is Laura Romero, and I can't wait for you to read her chapter. Laura has an enthusiasm for life that's infectious, is a mission-driven "sister" engaged in supporting numerous nonprofits and causes, and a kick-ass businesswoman. She's my kind of human, someone with whom I could easily share a couple bottles of good wine and plenty of laughs.

Laura naturally attracts people. The day before I interviewed her, she celebrated a milestone birthday. Two of her really dear friends and her parents hosted a party for her at a local bar with about sixty of Laura's closest friends in attendance. We're talking friends from grade school all the way through college and her twenty-year career in the tech industry, plus a few others she's met along the way. Yes, that's quite a bunch of peeps.

As she was sharing this info with me, I felt compelled to pose this question: How does someone attract such a large cadre of close friends? Most consider themselves quite lucky if they have one or two good pals.

Laura was a bit stumped. As is the case with most of us when it comes to our natural talents, Laura didn't readily see how incredible her abilities are. As I poked around further, I came to learn that she has been described as having a "PhD" in business relationships. A PhD?! That's a very effective descriptor for someone who has an advanced understanding of a certain subject matter. Even though there is no actual degree in cultivating business relationships, Laura could certainly teach a few classes in it. And from the number of folks at her recent soiree, evidently, she applies her natural talent in business-relationship building to her personal life as well!

Let's dive into Laura's chapter and get her take on how to cultivate strong and lasting business relationships, how you can benefit from working with a life coach, how to stay focused and even thrive when your company is in a state of flux, and more.

When Laura graduated from college with a degree in clothing and textiles and a minor in French, she had her sights set on becoming a clothing buyer and traveling the world, especially Paris. Laura is a self-described "unapologetic Francophile" and sports a Fleur De Lis tattoo to prove it. She has a strong affinity toward the French language, history, culture, and people, all of which she studied for years. Later in her career, she traveled to France on business and almost didn't come home. "I spent a long weekend just walking the streets of Paris, in thirty-degree November weather," she recalls. "I loved every minute of it—the culture, Christmas market, food, the sights, Champagne, and all the magic that Paris exudes."

Earlier in her career, business trips to Paris were not in the cards because Laura's career took off in a slightly different direction from what she had originally anticipated. She recognized remarkable success in United-States-based retail sales, design, and merchandising; worked for Macy's and The Gap; and opened the very first Old Navy store in California. Laura leaves this experience off her resume, though credits it for helping her hone her relationship development skills. "In retail, you deal with all walks of life—some bad, some good, and a little bit in between," Laura observes. "And it really refines you as a person by having to deal with a multitude of personalities."

But the retail way of life with long work hours, mostly on weekends, peppered with a liberal dose of holiday craziness, prompted Laura to leap from the retail to automotive industry when a position was offered to her. It was there that she became enamored with technology. "I found a job as an inside sales rep for a company that did sales for the automotive after-market. As part of my training, I worked in an auto parts store for three months and did work on cars. It was quite the departure from what I was doing previously, but I got to learn different technology applications, and in the process, became very interested in the industry. In August 1996, I started working as an inside sales rep with Oracle and have been entrenched ever since."

After her initial stint in inside sales, Laura elected to not go into direct sales. "I can sell, but I'm not a fan of it," she says. "I'm not the love 'em and leave 'em type of customer-relationship person. I prefer to develop, cultivate, manage, and farm a long-term relationship, and if I can leverage a business channel through that relationship, that's what I love."

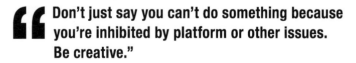 **Don't just say you can't do something because you're inhibited by platform or other issues. Be creative."**

When it comes to cultivating meaningful business channel partnerships, Laura recommends that women take the time to identify the business need for the potential partner first. It could be a technology or sales need, or a need to be able to transact business in an area that the company is currently not engaged. Second, she stresses the importance of doing your research to find complementary relationships that might make sense for the individual and his or her company. This means doing your homework to learn as much as you can about other technology companies—what they're doing, how they're evolving, what's their global impact, as well as the types of people who hold key leadership positions.

"A lot of times you might find potential partner companies that have some of the most fantastic technology in the world, but they don't necessarily make the best channel partners. You need to find a group of people who are collaborative, are willing to work through challenges, and look at the bigger picture to see where opportunities lie."

Laura continues, "Ultimately, you have to jointly build a plan to reach mutual success in driving a business. It's important to share ideas and be open with each other. Don't just say you can't do something because you're inhibited by platform or other issues. Be creative. Find ways to leverage the business partnership to create awareness together in the market, to foster thought leadership, and really put a footprint out there."

> **I document the positive experiences, those times when I've been able to move the needle forward in the relationship, and I document the more difficult experiences that were tough to navigate around."**

Laura recognizes that many business relationships click naturally, but not all. Some people are easier to gel with than others. She finds the more challenging behaviors include working with people who say "no" all the time without considering options, and those who are steadfast in their ways and unwilling to bend. Over the years, Laura has cultivated techniques that she uses to get to know all types of people, including those who may be more difficult to work with, that help cement strong business relationships.

"I create a file of information on each person and observe and document as much as I can, pulling out key points of how he or she ticks," Laura shares. "I document the positive experiences, those times when I've been able to move the needle forward in the relationship, and I document the more difficult experiences that were tough to navigate around." Laura processes the information by looking for patterns and preferences. She then uses her information to determine how best to communicate with the person to keep the business-relationship development process on track.

Laura also makes it a point to learn about people as individuals. She'll ask questions and have conversations on topics outside of work or a particular project. She's found that people enjoy talking about themselves, and she likes to listen. She also likes to uncover a shared connection with business associates and uses LinkedIn and Facebook regularly to get ideas on conversation starters and names of people in both her and the other person's network.

Yet with all her deliberative work to make relationships click, Laura knows when it's time to move on…and she does just that. "Sometimes I have to go as far as removing people from my professional network. It's not easy, but it's something I've had to learn how to do. You have to walk away from business relationships that don't make sense and any kind of negativity or people who are connected to that negativity that could potentially affect your reputation. That may sound a little harsh, it's just that life is too short. We can't waste air space connecting with people who suck the energy out of us."

Laura has learned much from being a woman in a male-dominated industry. "Being in tech teaches you how to have confidence and how to not take crap from people," she finds. "It's an exciting industry, and, as women, we bring a lot to the table. The negative people or events toughen you up so you can't let stuff bother you. Get over it and move on."

❝❝ We can't waste air space connecting with people who suck the energy out of us."

Moving on is very important to Laura, who believes all women need to keep paving the way and making a difference for themselves, each other, and those to come. Specifically, she has found that participating in women's groups, such as

Cloud Girls (cloudgirls.org), and working with a professional coach to be particularly effective.

Laura had a significant career breakthrough working with Chris Melching, executive communications and presentation coach with Center State Group and a Power Camp coach and facilitator. At the time, Laura was with a company where she felt significantly underpaid. She had been at the organization for thirteen years and performed well. But even her leadership couldn't close the gap in her salary. As is often—and unfairly—the case, new hires with little or no work experience were brought in for positions comparable to Laura's at a substantively higher base salary. The company policy was to not adjust salaries for existing staff accordingly. Still, Laura wasn't sure she wanted to leave because she was uncertain she had the skills another employer would want. Chris helped her turn that thinking around.

"I went to one of Chris's Power Camps. It's a corporate-level, three-day super intensive retreat where you do a lot of work to find your balance in life and anything else that is important to you. It's mentally exhausting, because she really challenges you, and it can get pretty emotional."

The retreat opened Laura's eyes to an important truth about herself—first, that she absolutely possessed the skills that another employer would want, and second, that these were skills for which other companies would pay her handsomely. She discovered that her extensive work experience gave her an excellent understanding of an array of technologies. And, just as important, she had gained real-world knowledge and skills in how to sell and develop business, how to be resourceful, and how to build a network. The fact was, during her thirteen-year tenure with her employer, she learned the key skills necessary to be successful in *any* industry.

When she returned to work after her Power Camp discoveries, she made the decision to get out of her comfort zone and take the career leap she knew she needed to make. She immediately reached out to her network to explore employment opportunities and worked with an experienced and well-respected resume writer.

❝❝ Make sure your resume and LinkedIn profile match."

Laura had not updated her resume in more than five years. It took three months of diligent work to review her past scorecards and refine her resume content to create a professional resume that put Laura's best foot forward. She also developed a system for documenting her accomplishments so that it wouldn't take so long to pull a future resume together if needed.

Laura recommends, "Make sure your resume and LinkedIn profile match. Our industry has been going through considerable changes and consolidation. You want to make sure you list all your positions and employers, even those that changed frequently due to mergers or acquisitions."

Laura's investment in career coaching and a resume writer paid off. When she left her company for a new opportunity, she was able to double her salary. She also credits her coach for giving her the tools to negotiate the best possible employment package. "My coach told me that when you have to negotiate your salary over the phone or in a video conference, don't rehearse it in front of a mirror. Instead, call yourself and leave a voicemail so you can hear how you sound. Don't talk to your script. This technique has worked for me every time."

Another piece of advice Laura offers up is how to operate when your company is in a state of flux, which is quite common for many who work in the technology sector. "It can be challenging for you if you don't know what the future looks like, and there's turmoil at your company. I get that. But you just have to let the executive team do their jobs, find out how you can support them, and not let the unknown distract you. You must stay focused on what you're doing and keep a pulse on what's going on in the industry. And keep those lines of communication open with recruiters in case they're needed."

" It can be challenging for you if you don't know what the future looks like, and there's turmoil at your company. I get that. But you just have to let the executive team do their jobs, find out how you can support them, and not let the unknown distract you."

There was a time in Laura's career when one of her previous employers announced a series of staff reductions. "There were twenty-six of us on the team that were part of the layoffs, and once it was communicated out, everyone started calling each other to commiserate. We were all experienced workers and just about every one of my colleagues was worried that they were too old to land another job. They were literally freaking out. They wanted to know why I wasn't freaking out with them. I told them 'I stay in contact with every single recruiter who calls me. I make sure I call them back or at least send a message whether I'm looking or not, and I forward their opportunities to others in my network. That relationship with recruiters helps me stay one step ahead.'"

She also reminded her colleagues to remember to value their work experience, as she learned to do, by finding a good career coach. "There is no college student who can just walk into a technology company and be successful in business development or sales. You can't learn that in school. You acquire that through experience. The tech industry is evolving rapidly and tech companies need experienced workers. You have to work your network and get that coach. That will be your saving grace."

> **And have your 'earthquake kit' packed and ready to go. That means have your updated resume completed, let recruiters know who you are, and cultivate a robust network of contacts and colleagues who could potentially link you to your next job."**

Laura encourages all women, even those who love their jobs and couldn't be any happier with their careers, to take the time to plan for the worst. "If a remotely interesting career opportunity comes your way, there is absolutely no reason why you can't have an interview, because you never know what might happen. And have your 'earthquake kit' packed and ready to go. That means have your updated resume completed, let recruiters know who you are, and cultivate a robust network of contacts and colleagues who could potentially link you to your next job. Then you'll feel better whether something happens or not."

Laura's wise words serve as a powerful reminder that the more prepared you are for any endeavor, the less worried you tend to be. And the less worried you are, the more attractive you become to your existing employer, as well as other great companies looking for someone terrific just like you.

A reader note: Six months after I interviewed Laura, she connected with me to share exciting news about a side business she co-founded—bon-faire.com. Bon Faire means "make good" in French. Together, Laura and her longtime friend Dana Leipold help women in midlife "make good" by stepping into their power and doing it in a way that benefits the world around them. They offer online courses, coaching, and live events. So, if you're over forty and you're ready to finally, yes finally, put yourself at the top of your to-do list and make a positive contribution, Bon Faire is perfect for you. If you're ready to put your decades of experience, skills, and knowledge to work in a way that empowers and energizes you, learn more about Bon Faire. Start by taking a free and fun quiz on the Bon Faire homepage so you can see what kind of Bon Faire woman you are right now. Yes, put this book down (it will take just a moment) and do it. It's a blast!

More about Laura Romero

Laura Romero has two decades of experience cultivating channel partner programs and global partnerships, as well as implementing strategies for delivering significant value and revenue while capturing market share across multiple industry sectors. She currently serves as a director, Global Partners and Programs at Plex Systems, Inc., where she is responsible for building the company's partner program from the ground up—her most challenging and thrilling role yet (plex.com).

At Plex, Laura is able to capitalize on the accumulation of her past work at Oracle, Taleo, and Dimension Data, leveraging longstanding partner and ERP ecosystem networks to build the framework to drive Cloud revenue while defining joint go-to-market pipeline development and deal-management initiatives. She also works with product management and strategy on roadmaps and the build/buy/partner strategies to position Plex solutions in the market.

In earlier roles, Laura has had success in driving company revenue through the channel by enabling System Integrators, SaaS Vendors, ISVs, Cloud Platform Vendors, Telcos, and distribution partners and captured significant revenue through the development and growth of ISV partner ecosystems.

When she's not crisscrossing North America to build partner relationships, you can find her exploring emerging markets and technical trends; advocating best practices and reference architectures; and building community consensus about the vast and dynamic cloud ecosystem through her work as an active board member of Cloud Girls, a women's technology organization (cloudgirls.org). Laura presents industry topics within this forum a few times a year.

A personal passion of Laura's is actively raising money for cancer research. She is a founding member and board director of the Terry Patters Memorial Foundation, Inc., supporting the UCSF Melanoma Center and previously, the Melanoma Research Foundation. Through these efforts she has contributed to more than $200,000 raised for melanoma treatments and research. She has previously served as a team captain supporting the annual Avon Foundation Walk for Breast Cancer and continues to donate to this formidable cause and others. She is an avid supporter of animal rescue organizations and an advocate for the bully breeds. She is proud to share that her rescued American Staffordshire Terrier ("pit bull"), Violet, received her AKC Canine Good Citizen certification and can be found accompanying Laura on her hiking, shopping, dining, and wine tasting excursions.

While she maintains her day job at Plex and board member responsibilities for Cloud Girls, in June of 2018, Laura embarked upon a new side venture with longtime friend and colleague Dana Leipold and co-founded Bon Faire, LLC. Bon Faire (bon-faire.com) is an online consulting services business and social enterprise targeting women in midlife who are frustrated in their current jobs and don't know how to take the leap into something new, gave up a career to raise a family and want to get back into the workforce, or have an idea or passion they'd like to turn into a business but don't know how. Laura is chief of business development.

Follow Laura on LinkedIn (Laura Romero) and Twitter (lhromero). She can also be contacted at lhromero@att.net.

CHAPTER 15

A Conversation with Theresa Caragol

Founder and CEO of Achieve Unite, LLC (achieveunite.com)

Inclusion and fairness in the workplace…is not simply
the right thing to do; it's the smart thing to do.
—Alexis Herman, American politician, 23rd United States
Secretary of Labor

The thing that always fascinated me about improv is
that it's basically a happy accident that you think you're
initiating.
—Tina Fey, American actress, comedian, writer,
producer, playwright

First, a Few of My Thoughts

If you have your sights set on becoming a leader in your organization, or a leader in your own life for that matter, I think you'll find tremendous value in this chapter. Our subject is a woman Google showcased in one of its famous landing-page photos—Theresa Caragol. The photo was of the top nine channel chiefs for 2011.

If you're thinking that Theresa was the only woman in that illustrious group, you'd be correct! This is a woman who is accustomed to being at the top—and often the only woman at the table. It's no surprise that she's a vocal advocate for inclusive leadership in the workplace. She believes that a more inclusive organizational culture has incredible power to dramatically increase profits for organizations and that diversity and inclusion have become mission-critical strategic tools for businesses today.

The time has certainly come for Theresa's type of forward-looking thinking.

Theresa also believes in happy accidents. When she told me about some of her experiences with happy accidents, I could relate. Theresa's happy accidents are, in my opinion, a byproduct of a particular skill she possesses. Theresa is open to what life presents her, and as you'll read in her chapter, it's a skill that has served her quite well.

Being open to what life presents us can be quite difficult. For me, it wasn't until I faced one of my fears—improvisational comedy—that I learned to be more open with what came my way in life. The Tina Fey quote I mentioned at the top of this chapter summed up the experience for me perfectly.

Before my foray into improv, I could best be described as a high-control type of gal. I had convinced myself that my fondness for control was why I was successful in my business career. But if I'm being totally honest with you, I knew that my insatiable need for being in control would only get me so far. I needed to be able to let go of the way I was achieving my outcomes. This realization prompted some soul searching, which led me to adopt a more philosophical approach. I was determined to be open to anything, attached to nothing. So, when a fellow acting chum of mine suggested I audition for an improvisational comedy troupe, I said "why not!"

I had never been interested in improv. To me, it was petrifying. I had success as a stage actress in college and as an adult. I enjoyed the process of memorizing lines, analyzing characters, and working out scenes. I found it easy and exhilarating. But improv? I found that nauseating. With improv I would need to fully let go of my tried and true cognitive processes, while working within a foreign framework complete with rules…and doing it all on the fly in front of an audience. Yikes! When an improv "game" worked, it really was a happy accident, just as Tina Fey described. I found that improv offered me numerous life lessons and helped me identify and appreciate more of my own happy accidents.

Back to Theresa: another one of her striking attributes is her passion for coaching and providing not only useful but transformative insights to others, especially women in the channel. In addition to her impressive academic education, she is a double-certified coach with credentials from the number-one recognized coach training resource—Coaching Training Institute—as well as the executive masters leadership program at Georgetown University. This added expertise makes her a triple threat in my book. She earned an MBA early in her career, because education credentials were important to her. She has a deep working knowledge of the technology and telecommunications industries, she knows what it takes to operate a business at all levels in the organization up to the very top of the org chart, and she marries all this with the added ability to drive performance even higher through the development of people and their potential.

I encourage you to spend some time exploring her website (achieveunite.com), including her blogs over the years. We're talking about some seriously astounding insights from a proven leader with a penchant for inspiring others. I promise it will be time well spent!

"If you let life present itself to you, amazing opportunities will happen," recommends Theresa. "I've had my share of happy accidents—experiences and opportunities that have come to me very organically and naturally that have turned into something special."

When Theresa graduated from Virginia Tech, she fell into tech by accident. After searching her college's employment opportunities board, she landed a job in Chicago at IBM. Because she excelled in that opportunity, she was presented another opportunity and went to work for Bay Networks.

"I remember being a sales rep for Bay Networks in Illinois and Wisconsin and opening up this magazine called CRN," says Theresa. "I was looking at this group of men called 'channel chiefs' and thought 'if they can do that, I can do that, too.'"

And she did.

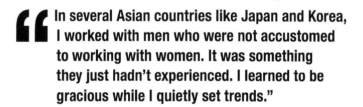

In several Asian countries like Japan and Korea, I worked with men who were not accustomed to working with women. It was something they just hadn't experienced. I learned to be gracious while I quietly set trends."

Theresa had always been driven and ambitious. When she set her mind to something, she was not deterred. She knew early in her career that she wanted to have a seat at the senior executive table. She didn't care one bit that she was the only woman in the room or that she'd selected a male-dominated industry on which to make her mark. She was focused, most clearly, on high performance and results.

Theresa reflects, "I was afforded my first global executive job in my early thirties and then continued to build my career with Nortel, then Ciena, and then Extreme Networks. As a global channel leader, I had the privilege of having an amazing career while traveling all over the world, conducting business and building partnerships in more than seventy different countries."

"In several Asian countries like Japan and Korea, I worked with men who were not accustomed to working with women. It was something they just hadn't experienced. I learned to be gracious while I quietly set trends. I absorbed so much knowledge and networked with remarkable people, many of whom are still my friends and colleagues today."

Living the life of a channel chief, however, did come with a unique set of challenges. Theresa traveled 90 percent of the time, which she didn't blink twice at because that was the job. When her first son was born, he and the Nanny traveled all over the world with her—13 countries, 39 states, and 206 flights—but once he entered kindergarten, traveling together was not in the cards and the logistics of life became a bit more difficult. When Theresa's second son was born with early health issues, she found herself at a crossroad.

"I always loved the work," she says. "It was the travel that posed a challenge. It's tough to do a trip to Asia in three days. You need at least a week. It started to get really challenging for me. My second son had some health challenges, and I didn't have the luxury of a stay-at-home husband to help care for our children. Things worked out for the best though. I had the courage to gracefully step down from my position and negotiate an incredible exit package that lasted about nine months. Life then presented itself with yet another happy accident."

> ❝ **I believe that partnering is a core tenet for business success. Yet good partnering is not easy. It's a real leadership competency that needs to be developed."**

Theresa began to take on independent consulting assignments, and it occurred to her if the men she knew were able to start their own consulting businesses, she could as well, and Achieve Unite was born. Founded by Theresa in 2016, Achieve Unite's consultancy services and business programs transform organizations leveraging revenue growth through building strategic alliances and partnerships.

Theresa's passion for Achieve Unite's people and business solutions shines brightly. "I just love the journey of building an entity that has its own culture and DNA," she says. "And I love the work we're doing. I believe that partnering is a core tenet for business success. Yet good partnering is not easy. It's a real leadership competency that needs to be developed. We have an assessment tool that helps executives uncover how they're doing in their partnering relationships, as well as opportunities to make dramatic improvements. Our work is at the forefront, and it genuinely excites me."

Theresa also feels strongly that leadership is a learned behavior. While there are many leadership practices to consider, she has found three to be particularly effective, and she offers leadership programs based on ACE: Leadership by Influence. It stands for authentic leadership, collaboration, and empowering others. "In my experience, as a leader you need to learn to engage in mentoring and sponsoring relationships; invest in yourself and others; be an inclusive leader; and take others along on your journey." It's also imperative that you regularly negotiate your employment package and make sure your compensation needs are met. This means not only your compensation—it's the whole package, including compensation, benefits, promotions, education, and new opportunities.

> **❝❝ You don't have to wait for a formal or informal mentoring program. Where you see talent, as either a mentor's or mentee's, cultivate spontaneous connections. Start small. Ask a question. Ask for an opinion. Ask for help."**

Theresa speaks and writes regularly on the topic of mentoring. Recently, she and her team published a blog outlining twelve ideas for succeeding in a mentoring relationship. Among the terrific ideas mentioned is this useful nugget: take mentoring as your personal responsibility. "You don't have to wait for a formal or informal mentoring program," notes Theresa. "Where you see talent, as either a mentor's or mentee's, cultivate spontaneous connections. Start small. Ask a question. Ask for an opinion. Ask for help. Rapport can be built in many ways, and often those organic or informal connections can yield as much success as formal programs."

Theresa recognizes that while more women today are engaging in mentoring relationships, not as many understand or have experience with sponsoring. Whereas mentoring can be more passive, sponsoring is more direct. "When I sponsor someone, I'm putting my name behind that person," Theresa emphasizes. "I'm telling my buddy Bob to hire Jessica, because she's excellent at what she does. I'm advocating for Jessica, while encouraging Bob to give an opportunity to a woman I know will do well for his company. If others had not sponsored me in the past, I would have never had the opportunities I had."

The second essential leadership practice Theresa recommends is to be able to create opportunities for yourself, especially when your pay is involved. "You've got to be able to negotiate the financial aspects related to your career, from your salary to your exit package," she urges. "I'm not going to lie and say this is easy. It can be challenging. You have to learn to get out of your comfort zone and take care of yourself."

Theresa related a story from earlier in her career when she was the only member on her company's leadership team who wasn't a vice president. She was also among the lowest paid. She met with the leader of human resources and her immediate executive and spoke with them about the business and why providing equal pay for equal work would be an advantage to the company. She then shared her personal goals for her own growth and development and how that supported the company's goals. The conversation was all about business. She didn't make it about herself, and she stripped out her personal emotions. She negotiated a new title and a compensation package that was on equal terms with other senior executives. She also earned a healthy dollop of respect and bolstered her credibility as a business executive as well.

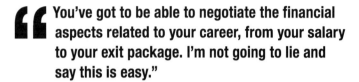 **You've got to be able to negotiate the financial aspects related to your career, from your salary to your exit package. I'm not going to lie and say this is easy."**

The third practice Theresa suggests women consider in their leadership development is to make it a priority to invest in your professional growth. She talks about four buckets of skills necessary to be successful today—1) soft skills, including emotional intelligence; 2) overall business acumen skills, including a solid working knowledge of finance, economics, operations, marketing, sales, and service; 3) specific business skills, relating to your particular area of expertise; and 4) technical skills, enabling you to get your work done in an efficient and effective manner.

Among these four areas of skill development, Theresa is adamant that investing in your soft skills education, especially EI, is more important than ever. "I do a tremendous amount of work around EI and helping others develop strong EI skills. The research supports that EI skills contribute to 80 percent of our success. EI is something you can develop—when you work it, it works!"

A fourth leadership practice that Theresa endorses is to nurture the qualities necessary to become an inclusive leader. "Being an inclusive leader means you create a workplace culture where employees feel connected and supported," she says. "Inclusive leaders foster innovation and creativity, and an opportunity for everyone to advance and thrive within the organization."

In her blog *The Power and Profitability of Woman in Tech* she sets forth four attributes of an inclusive leader:

1.   **Empowerment**—Inclusive leaders encourage team members to solve problems, not just do a job. They want their team to have new ideas and develop skills that will empower them to be a better resource for the whole organization.

2.   **Accountability**—Inclusive leaders are confident in their team. They don't micro-manage but, instead, hold them responsible for their performance. They let them own the responsibilities and have control over the outcomes.

3.   **Humility**—Inclusive leaders are open to input and feedback. They can admit mistakes and learn from them. They will know their own limitations and seek assistance from others to overcome challenges and be successful.

4.   **Courage**—Inclusive leaders will put aside their personal interests to achieve what needs to be done. They are not afraid to do what is right and will often take some risks to ensure the correct outcome.

The fifth recommendation Theresa shares with women interested in becoming leaders is to learn to take others along on their journeys—those with whom you work and those closest to you. "It feels like we've entered into the 'Age of the Woman,'" Theresa observes. "You can sense that many wonderful opportunities for women are right around the corner. What rubs me the wrong way, though, is when we exclude others from being a part of our journey. This is not a women-only movement. We need to bring everybody along, especially men. There are many, many men who are supportive and genuinely interested in assisting women as they achieve their goals. We must be careful to not alienate others. All people matter."

> **You can sense that many wonderful opportunities for women are right around the corner. What rubs me the wrong way, though, is when we exclude others from being a part of our journey. This is not a women-only movement. We need to bring everybody along, especially men."**

"I learned this the hard way. I had been overly focused on metrics and outcomes as the primary determinants of success. Over time, it became apparent to me that success in business and life is tied to your success with people, especially those closest to you. I was so focused on my career and sons that I didn't even see that I was sacrificing the relationship with my partner. That was a raw lesson to learn. You can't over-rotate to one extreme. I don't think it's a matter of balance; quite frankly, I don't believe in balance. It's about integration and attitude. You have to focus on all of the most important things—including him."

"My grandma is one hundred years old and absolutely amazing," says Theresa. "For as long as I can remember, she would tell me that attitude is everything. And she lives this advice to this day. She has no cartilage in her knees, and yet she refuses to use a wheelchair because she believes if she goes in a wheelchair she will lose her independence. Her independence matters to her, so she integrates walking into each day even though it's hard as hell."

Now that's a testament to the power of attitude and integration. Thanks, Grandma. And thank you, Theresa.

More about Theresa Caragol

Theresa Caragol is founder and CEO of Achieve Unite, LLC, a strategic advisory and performance partnering firm that provides business acceleration services to global enterprises including partner and channel development, go-to-market planning, merger and acquisition channel integration, and executive learning forums (achieveunite. com). She has more than twenty years' experience in building and managing multimillion-dollar indirect channel teams and strategic alliance business and programs from inception to sales success. Prior to founding Achieve Unite, Theresa held senior executive roles at Extreme Networks, Ciena, and Nortel.

Theresa is passionate about coaching employees and mentoring young people into STEM fields. She is honored to be one of fifteen women selected for the First Leadership Foundry in Washington, DC—an organization dedicated to mentoring and recruiting women for positions on corporate boards. Theresa has received numerous IT industry channel accolades recognizing her work including: 2014 CRN Top 50 Most Influential Channel Chiefs, 2013 CRN Top 10 Next Generation Channel Leaders, and 2015 Golden Bridge Gold Award for Best Program Leader.

Theresa graduated with honors from Virginia Tech University. She has an MBA from the University of Wisconsin's Lubar School of Business and holds an executive master's degree in leadership from Georgetown University's McDonough School of Business.

Follow Theresa on LinkedIn (Theresa Caragol) and Twitter (TheresaCaragol). She can also be contacted at theresa@ theresacaragol.com.

CHAPTER 16

A Conversation with Rebecca Rosen

Vice President of Marketing, Broadvoice (broadvoice.com)

Emotional intelligence is a way of recognizing, understanding, and choosing how we think, feel, and act. It shapes our interactions with others and our understanding of ourselves. It defines how and what we learn; it allows us to set priorities; it determines the majority of our daily actions. Research suggests it is responsible for as much as 80 percent of the success in our lives.

—J. Freedman, author, specialist on Emotional Intelligence, Chief Executive Officer of Six Seconds

First, a Few of My Thoughts

Our heroine for this chapter is Rebecca Rosen. If you're like me, you will be inspired by her life lessons and how she's applied them throughout her career. Oh, and be prepared to have a mind-altering experience. That's not hyperbole, my friends.

After I ended my first interview call with Rebecca, I just sat there for a moment—motionless. I was excited and a bit overwhelmed. I was processing. I also asked myself "what just happened?"

You see, there is something about talking with Rebecca that is simply spellbinding. She's a unicorn—a rare and magical creature—yet there is nothing mythical about her. She's the real deal.

From my vantage point as a colossal geek when it comes to the topic of Emotional Intelligence (EI), Rebecca's particular magic power is her ability to identify and manage her own emotions and the emotions of others. Plus, her ability to self-assess allows her to apply her emotional understanding to tasks like making choices and problem solving. If you think that sounds easy, I can assure you it is not.

Right from the start of our interview, I was immediately struck by her quiet strength and old-soul wisdom. When the interview ended and I revived myself, I swiftly transcribed every word from our conversation. At night I couldn't sleep as the interview swirled about in my subconscious, and in the morning when I awoke, I promptly emailed Rebecca a request to interview her again to ask a few more questions. I just had to find out how she got so darn emotionally intelligent. I had to know because EI is something most of us mere mortals have to laboriously strive for and painstakingly develop, and this woman had it in spades.

When I interviewed Rebecca the second time, she explained how early guidance from her parents helped shape her responses to pivotal moments throughout her life, and in the process, helped her to further develop her emotional intelligence. By so generously sharing her personal stories in this chapter, Rebecca is giving us a wondrous gift. Because even if you didn't have the same positive influences early in your life, you can get that guidance, right now, in the words that follow.

Rebecca has a real passion for learning, which she likens to playing a game of chess. She anticipates other people's responses, as well as her next best move. She projects into the future how things can play out, and if something goes wrong, she digs in to learn why it went wrong, what role she played, and how she can improve further.

Rebecca does not blame others or point fingers. If anything, her first inclination is to take ownership. "I actually believe that most things that do not go as planned are my fault," she laughs. "So even when I know that the fault may lie elsewhere, I would much rather jump on the grenade and take responsibility for whatever went sideways so that we can come back to the table and talk things out."

Throughout her life, Rebecca has felt that she has a capability to see when emotions are getting the best of people and situations. She can actually sense when emotions are taking over, causing people to focus on arguing rather than the business objective they're trying to accomplish. She credits her parents for helping her develop this sense of knowing, as well as learning other pivotal lessons in emotional intelligence.

> **Later, after we left, he said 'sometimes you have to let people go through their own process to be able to get to where you want to end up.'"**

One lesson Rebecca relates was the first time she was buying a new car. She asked her dad to accompany her to the dealership. The gentleman they worked with was the embodiment of just about every bad story you could imagine about working with a car salesperson. The gentleman did not address her, and he didn't listen to the fact that she already knew which car she wanted and was ready to buy. Instead, rather than answering her questions, he proceeded to launch into a full-blown sales spiel. "I was getting so aggravated," Rebecca says. "At some point, I remember my father laid his hand on my hand to tell me to chill out. Later, after we left, he said 'sometimes you have to let people go through their own process to be able to get to where you want to end up.'"

Rebecca's father, a business consultant, modeled his consultative approach he used with the car salesperson quite often throughout Rebecca's formative years. It resonated so much with her that she adopted it as her own workstyle preference even though she's an employee and not an outside consultant. Rebecca truly sees that a part of her job is to provide independent counsel to her employer. As such, she feels responsible for giving her employer the best of her feedback regardless of whether they want to act on it or not. Plus, like a consultant, when she shares her ideas she doesn't get too attached to them. That way, if her employer chooses to not put her ideas into play, she doesn't feel slighted. She feels satisfied, knowing that she gave them the best of her thinking at that time.

To offer recommendations and ask support for your ideas is another value Rebecca inherited from her parents. "My mother taught me to be courageous, to ask questions of people, even strangers, and to advocate for my own ideas. It's something I teach my ten-year-old twins. There are certain discussions that they can have with their teachers right now. For instance, I'm not going to call a teacher on behalf of my children because they got a question wrong on a test that they thought they had right. I want my children to feel that they can walk up to the teacher and respectfully advocate for their own positions."

On the flipside, Rebecca learned that in the process of advocating for her own ideas, she also has to be open to other ways or viewpoints. When she was looking for graduate schools, her area of focus was technology-based dance choreography. As is the case with any advanced degree in the arts, she had to choose the schools she wanted to attend and audition for admission. Then, based on that audition, the school would either select her or not and provide scholarship funding…or not. Rebecca's father told her that he would not pay her way to travel around the country to audition for the schools that interested her. Instead, the schools would have to accept her first. Once she was accepted, he would pay for her to tour the two or three in which she was most interested.

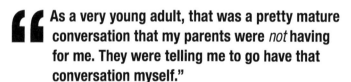

As a very young adult, that was a pretty mature conversation that my parents were *not* having for me. They were telling me to go have that conversation myself."

One of the universities that accepted Rebecca provided her a very prestigious scholarship. They offered her what was essentially a paid faculty position, in addition to paying her tuition, room, and board. But Rebecca had her heart set on another university—Arizona State—because they had a world-renowned think tank for research in art and technology. However, Arizona State University only offered her a $500 scholarship.

When she shared the news with her father, he told her that if she wanted to go to Arizona State, she had to negotiate for the same offer the other university gave her. "Who negotiates for graduate school? Who does that?!" Rebecca muses. "I got on the phone with the university. I told them I won this other prestigious scholarship and the only way I would accept their offer was if they matched it. And they matched it. As a very young adult, that was a pretty mature conversation that my parents were *not* having for me. They were telling me to go have that conversation myself."

Rebecca attained her master's degree and was absolutely fascinated with the creative projects she produced while at Arizona State. She was able to work with others in the think tank across multiple disciplines to choreograph technology-integrated dance and other multimedia artistic expressions. After graduate school, she was offered a wonderful opportunity and moved to California to work with a well-known choreographer. But that experience was not a good fit for her, and her bank account was dwindling. Rebecca found it was time for her to seek other employment. After a short stint with a nonprofit, her university and work experience served her quite well when she launched her next career with a tech company.

"Being a choreographer and working on complex technology-integrated productions gave me a very interesting perspective," relates Rebecca. "First, you have to be able to see the whole field and how that field interacts with the other areas. Second, you have to understand or look at things from a process perspective because when you do one thing it impacts how something else happens later on. Third, you have to learn to manage the talent you have, find out what they can do that's great, and then project that out to create something that is extraordinary."

Rebecca has been able to build on her experiences throughout her career. She now runs marketing for a software services company where she has responsibility for the traditional side of marketing, which keeps her creative brain engaged, as well as product management, which allows her to flex her analytical abilities. In product management, she's responsible for product research and innovation. Rebecca immerses herself in the product to understand all of its possibilities and benefits and to develop a vision for future products, focusing on what a product could look like and how it could help customers do something better, be more productive, and create more revenue. "I love being able to be a part of my company's story and contribute to our growth, whether it's in number of leads or bottom-line revenue generation. I believe there is always something to be passionate about and to take ownership of—both in the company, in general, and in the products when they're released. I can say 'I had a hand in that,' which I find super exciting, too."

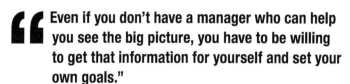 **Even if you don't have a manager who can help you see the big picture, you have to be willing to get that information for yourself and set your own goals."**

Feeling a sense of ownership at work is important to Rebecca, and she has a few recommendations for women to consider. "I think so many people feel disenfranchised because they don't understand the contribution they're making to the business or how that contribution is positively impacting the business. Even if you don't have a manager who can help you see the big picture, you have to be willing to get that information for yourself and set your own goals."

To illustrate this point further, Rebecca provided an example of how an entry-level customer service representative in a call center could cultivate a sense of ownership. Call centers often display wall boards of information showing reps how they're performing against various metrics—from actual and average handle times, to call escalations and first-call resolution. Call center reps need to understand how their performance impacts the whole business. They can then look at their own performance to determine what they could do better and then monitor their performance over time—month over month, quarter over quarter—and set goals to improve. As Rebecca sees it, "If you know how you are personally impacting your organization, that makes you feel as if you're a part of something bigger than yourself, and it makes you feel proud of your accomplishments."

> **If you're early in your career, you may not be at the point where you get to participate in more strategic conversations. What can you do then? You can do great work."**

When you're in business, another great piece of advice is to remember that results matter. Ultimately, that's how businesses are measured. Rebecca shares another memorable lesson learned: "In my early thirties, there was an incident at work where we had made public some key information that was not supposed to be shared yet, and there was the potential for some significant negative consequences. I remember calling my boss at the time, in tears, asking him if I was going to lose my job. And his response to me was 'that's not the right question right now; the right question right now is *what do we do to resolve this situation?*' That was such good feedback for me because the first response was very selfish. The second response was an actual approach to finding a solution. The second response showed a desire for results over self."

Rebecca also recommends that even if you don't always understand the big picture, you still can do something just as impactful and totally in your control. "If you're early in your career, you may not be at the point where you get to participate in more strategic conversations. What can you do then? You can do great work. And that's what people will remember about you. I find that you cross so many paths that your network is important. Who you're working with today isn't going to be who you're working with tomorrow. Yet, who you work with today will be able to introduce you to your next opportunity tomorrow. If you do good work, respect other people, and treat people kindly, that's going to take you far in your career."

> **❝ I am totally willing to be the dumbest person in the room. If people start talking about technology or tech processes that I've never heard of before, I'm willing to ask questions to learn as much as I can."**

Rebecca also stresses the importance of being curious, observing those around you, and asking plenty of questions. She has found that the smartest people she's known can take the most difficult concepts and make them really simple. They're able to explain things in a way that is easy to understand, and they articulate what they're sharing in very basic, street-level language. To get to that point, you have to able to observe what's happening around you and ask questions. "I'm always super inquisitive, and I think, quite frankly, that's one of the reasons I've gotten as far as I have," she says. "I am totally willing to be the dumbest person in the room. If people start talking about technology or tech processes that I've never heard of before, I'm willing to ask questions to learn as much as I can. Remember, you are not the only person in the room who has those questions."

Additionally, another attribute worth developing is your ability to take the emotion out of a conversation and present the facts, as well as the cause and effect of those facts. "As soon as any person, male or female, starts to become emotional, everybody shuts down from that conversation," finds Rebecca. She suggests some positive approaches to help you get out of that emotional moment. You can talk about why something matters or is important. You can examine what behaviors you may be demonstrating that could give you a more favorable result.

"Let's say people are going around the room and listening to feedback, and for some reason you feel like your feedback isn't being heard by the group. You have two options. You can point fingers at everyone else, or you can look at your own communication style and ask if you're being effective. If you've done that questioning and your answer is 'no,' that's an opportunity to do something positive to address that challenge. You have to own it."

Rebecca also believes women have to own what happens to them in the workplace, including instances of harassment or not feeling welcome in certain situations. "We have to be willing to speak up for ourselves in a way that's respectful and gets action."

> **When somebody isn't treating you right and you're not getting your needs met, remember that is not the only employer out there. That is not representative of every experience you're going to have."**

Rebecca found Courtney Farrell's TED Talk, "Girl Up: The Secrets to an Extraordinary Life," to be particularly instructive. (Checkout the fifteen-minute video for yourself on YouTube.) In the video, Courtney talks about how women are taught to aspire to perfection even though it's not an attainable quality for any human. She encourages women, especially those ages seventeen through twenty-four, to step into their power, knowing that it's enough to show up with self-confidence and love. She also talks about what to do if someone isn't meeting your needs—you tell them so and break up with them.

"A lot of times when I hear people talk about women in technology, it's not that young women, and women in general, aren't interested in being in technology. It's more that they may have had a first job or experience in tech that wasn't a friendly one," says Rebecca. "But that doesn't mean that's the only job or experience that exists. There are great environments and great cultures. You just might be in one that isn't meeting your needs."

Rebecca continues, "The challenge is when you're young, you may have a mortgage, college loans, and other expenses, so you may find it hard to 'break up with' your employer. It's a lot like when you know you need to break up with a boyfriend, but you don't want to because you're really scared that you're never going to find that next boyfriend or partner. Or if they break up with you, you're afraid you'll never find love again. But we know that's not true. The same applies when you have a job. When somebody isn't treating you right and you're not getting your needs met, remember that is not the only employer out there. That is not representative of every experience you're going to have. You've got to make the break."

You've got to Girl Up.

More about Rebecca Rosen

Rebecca Rosen is vice president of marketing at Broadvoice, an award-winning provider of hosted voice, unified communications, and SIP Trunking services for businesses (broadvoice.com). As the leader of Broadvoice's marketing efforts, she was instrumental in the roll-out of Broadvoice b-hive, a unified communications-as-a-service (UCaaS) and virtual contact center platform that enables channel partners to deliver unprecedented cloud communications capabilities to SMBs nationwide.

In May of 2018, Rebecca was named by CRN©, a brand of The Channel Company, to its prestigious 2018 Women of the Channel list. The executives who comprise this annual list span the IT channel, representing vendors, distributors, solution providers, and other organizations that figure prominently in the channel ecosystem. Rebecca was recognized for her outstanding leadership, vision, and unique role in driving channel growth and innovation. She has also been recognized for her channel leadership as a recipient of the Channel Partners 2018 Circle of Excellence Award.

Rebecca is an accomplished technology marketing executive with more than seventeen years of experience serving competitive communications providers. She also is vice president and chair of the Finance Committee for Alliance of Channel Women (formerly Women in the Channel); a former faculty member for leading IT industry association CompTIA; and a frequent speaker on marketing, strategy, leadership, and technology issues at industry events. Rebecca earned a master of fine arts degree from Arizona State University and a bachelor of fine arts from George Mason University in Virginia.

Follow Rebecca on LinkedIn (Rebecca Rosen) and Twitter (RebeccaMRosen). She can also be contacted at rebeccar@ broadvoice.com.

CHAPTER 17 _____

A Conversation with Nancy Ridge

Executive Vice President, Telecom Brokers (telecombrokers.com) and
Co-Founder of Alliance of Channel Women (allianceofchannelwomen.org)

_____

> Life is not merely a series of meaningless
> accidents or coincidences. But rather, it is a
> tapestry of events that culminate in an exquisite,
> sublime plan.
> —*Serendipity*, The Film

> Transformation lives in accountability.
> —Patricia McDade, American business person

First, a Few of My Thoughts

Serendipity. Fate. Providence.

Have you ever heard or used these expressions when you experienced something in your life? Pay attention to what's happening when you do. Pay *very* close attention. Here's my recent story of when "serendipity" and our chapter focus, Nancy Ridge, collided.

Let me contextualize this for you.

It was the summer of 2018. I was knee-deep in customizing one of my emotional intelligence leadership training programs, working on another client's communications effort, establishing my own nonprofit focused on self-empowerment for women and youth, promoting a new book of mine published earlier in the year, and writing this book. It was an exhilarating, if not a tad exhausting, time!

One night I'm casually catching up on LinkedIn, and this post grabs my attention. It's a link to a Forbes article by Geri Stengel titled *How Women Angels are Good for Innovation and the Economy.* The woman sharing the article posted these words "... women see market opportunities that men pass by. To open up new markets, bring out new products and get strong companies off the ground, we need more women angels (investors)."

I felt compelled to comment, "So elegantly stated! I agree and have found that women spot trends with amazing agility and speed, seeing important connections and knowing just what to do to take meaningful action."

Fast-forward a couple of weeks. One of my "women angels" Tanya Youvan, who has invested in me by supporting my work, mentions that she'd like to share a copy of my book with her CEO. I tell her I will mail her a few books and sign one specifically for her CEO. She asks if I can sign a second book for a close friend of her CEO's. I happily send off the signed books.

Fast-forward a couple more weeks. I join the Alliance of Channel Women (www.allianceofchannelwomen.org). This was a no-brainer for me. Over the preceding months, I interviewed fifteen different women in tech and wrote their amazing stories, which you've been reading about in this book. What do these women have in common you may ask? Many of them are part of the Alliance of Channel Women. So, I become a member and begin to get immersed in their operation (they do an amazing job of welcoming and acclimating new members). Before long, I start to get involved in a couple of their committees.

The day-to-day work of the Alliance is powered by Basecamp—an online project-management system. One day I get an email generated from Basecamp that says "Nancy Ridge just set up an account for you. All you need to do is choose a username and password..." I easily set up my account and send off a quick thank you.

I get back this response "You're so welcome! I'm thrilled you've decided to join (the Alliance). I love your book and the stories. Deb Ward gave me a copy with your very own signature inside! I've done the *7 Circles* [an exercise featured in the book] with the ladies on my staff, and we are finding great insight and opportunity through the process. If you would ever like to consider my story, I would be honored to share. I hope to meet you soon!"

What?!

The connection hits me squarely. Finally, right? Nancy Ridge is the close friend of Tanya's CEO, Deb Ward. Nancy Ridge is the "Nancy" whom I signed a book for that Deb hand-delivered. Nancy Ridge is the woman who posted the LinkedIn "angel investors" article I commented on. Nancy Ridge is the co-founder of the Alliance of Channel Women. This is *the* Nancy Ridge.

I responded to Nancy, "Thank you for your very kind email. I'm thrilled to hear that you enjoyed the book, found value in it, and put it into action with your team! It would be my honor to share your story in my newest book project..."

Nancy sent me this note back, "Wow. I have to tell you this email arrived while I was meeting with my staff going over the results of their *7 Circles* work—what they are each committed to. How is that for serendipity? I would LOVE to participate in your book and get to know you in the process."

Serendipity.

Less than a week later, Nancy and I had our interview for this book chapter. It was nothing short of spectacular.

Nancy and I easily talked about dozens of topics. She is a true champion for you and cares about your journey. Heck, she established a successful nonprofit for women in technology!

When our call ended, I just sat there for a moment, unable to speak.

Then "serendipity" struck again.

After spending a summer working on client projects in emotional intelligence leadership and writing the stories for this book where it became clear that emotional intelligence was a common thread, the universe gave me the perfect example of an emotionally intelligent leader in action—Nancy Ridge. And what an ideal way to end section one of this book and transition into the second section, which is all about how you can become a more emotionally intelligent leader…of yourself and in your own life right now.

Serendipity. Fate. Providence.

In other words—it's meant to be.

Nancy Ridge is a revered and passionate advocate and industry thought leader for women in technology. She uses her voice to be part of a collective conversation so that the next generation of girls and women who love tech, as she does, will reach new heights and, ultimately, change the world.

She cares deeply about helping women rise into their own power as business leaders and provides inspiration, support, and practical, actionable guidance through the Alliance of Channel Woman, a nonprofit she co-founded in 2010 specifically for women in technology. She also recognizes women are at a pivotal point in history and that situations may actually get worse before they get better. But they will continue to improve, although at times it may feel we advance two steps forward, one step back.

"I have and continue to deal with the challenges of being a woman in the tech world," says Nancy. "I have suffered sexual abuse and harassment. I have been paid less than my male colleagues even when I've outperformed them. My role as sole breadwinner for my family has made me vulnerable to accepting employment agreements that didn't serve me well. I have been talked over, passed over, and told to be quiet. Yet, I am not defeated."

> You must remember that circumstances, even if they aren't the ones you want, are there to help you be stronger so you can press on. Now, more than ever, you must stay positive and focused on your purpose."

Far from it. Above all else, Nancy knows what comes from the power of hope…and action.

"My deepest desire is for all woman to have hope and to not give up," says Nancy. "You must remember that circumstances, even if they aren't the ones you want, are there to help you be stronger so you can press on. Now, more than ever, you must stay positive and focused on your purpose."

And as Nancy has come to know, your purpose matters because it's closely aligned with what matters most to you. While there are many lessons Nancy learned over her impressive career, among the most impactful were the lessons she learned in the areas of mentorship and negotiation. These lessons helped connect her to and keep her focused on her purpose, and they helped her not only to survive but to thrive in her career.

> **We say, 'If I want something done, I have to do it myself' or 'I don't need anybody, I can go it alone.' We think we're showing strength, but we're not. These isolating statements are lies and can be quite damaging."**

Nancy sees mentorship as one of the best ways to break the isolation that many women often experience in business. Women may feel isolated because of the numerous demands placed upon them and the high expectations that usually come with those demands. Isolation not only hurts women, but it perpetuates an unhealthy competition among women. It's important to recognize why you isolate yourself so you can shift your thinking. "Sometimes we isolate ourselves because we've been disappointed by people," reflects Nancy. "We might have asked them to do something and they either don't do it or do it right. We say, 'If I want something done, I have to do it myself' or 'I don't need anybody, I can go it alone.' We think we're showing strength, but we're not. These isolating statements are lies and can be quite damaging."

When you form a mentoring relationship, you break down the walls of isolation. You get to know another person, and they get to know you. But before a mentoring relationship can flourish, you have to be vulnerable, and this can be difficult for some women.

"To make the most out of a mentoring relationship, you have to drop your ego and admit you need help. You have to admit there are others who know more about things than you do. And know your motives for being mentored. If your motives are to move forward, grow, make an impact, contribute something new, or be happier in your career, those are pure motives. If your motives are to gain an advantage without admitting you need assistance because you're afraid of being 'found out,' there's a good chance your mentoring experience will be hampered."

When you drop your ego, you'll also be in a better position to attract the right mentor to you. Nancy recommends paying attention to people who have a skill you wish to polish further or desire but currently don't have, or people who excite you. Let your natural curiosity about that person lead you to asking him or her to serve as your mentor.

> **We can be these really forward-thinking, modern women, but we still have this conditioning belief that being committed to activities that benefit others is more important than being committed to something like mentoring, which benefits us directly."**

Curiosity is exactly what led Nancy to finding some extraordinary mentors, including Patricia McDade, who has since passed, whose quote is featured at the beginning of this chapter. But it was one of Nancy's first mentors who helped inform her thinking of how to be a woman in technology. Here's the backstory. After high school, Nancy took a full-time job to support herself and pay for college at Wayne State in Detroit. She landed a secretarial position with Honeywell and was immediately propelled into a world of technological innovation where multimillion dollars deals were made and she worked closely behind the scenes with the executives and sales teams that closed those deals.

A few years into her career with Honeywell, Nancy began working in their microchip division and was introduced to the Silicon Valley and the exploding world of microprocessors, Original Equipment Manufacturers, distributors, and channel sales. Nancy worked for a dynamic woman executive and was immediately drawn to her ability to create effective distribution channels, as well as to her technology prowess. The woman was also very attractive and, in a time when women dressed like men to fit it, she was feminine and comfortable in her own skin. These characteristics were quite compelling to Nancy, and when the woman left Honeywell to become a leader at a start-up tech company, Nancy decided to interview at the same company.

"I pursued that job to follow this amazing woman executive. I wanted to be in close proximity to a role model and mentor, and I told her so during our interview. The experience did not disappoint. She was one of the big influencers in my life."

From Nancy's perspective, accountability is crucial to making the most of the mentoring experience. It also requires a commitment to the mentoring process and all it entails. She finds that it's easier for women to make commitments on behalf of others than it is to make commitments on behalf of themselves. "We can be these really forward-thinking, modern women, but we still have this conditioning belief that being committed to activities that benefit others is more important than being committed to something like mentoring, which benefits us directly."

> ❝ It's unrealistic to say you're going to get a mentor, and in sixty days your life will change dramatically. That's a sure way to set yourself up for disappointment."

Inherent in being committed to mentoring is being consistent. Nancy finds that often women tend to contact their mentors sporadically or when something goes wrong and they need a dumping ground. That's not how mentorship works. What you put in is definitely what you get out. Talk to your mentor frequently, and keep them engaged in your career development.

And above all else, remember that when you enter a mentoring relationship, you're entering a *two-way* relationship. "In a mentoring relationship, you get to know each other," Nancy reminds. "It's not all about you. You have to be willing to show an interest in that person's life and to be open to their feedback and listen to what they have to say."

She continues, "Mentoring has given me a fast-track in my career in many ways. It's helped me learn things that I would never have learned in college. At the same time though, it's very much a slow and unfolding process. It's unrealistic to say you're going to get a mentor, and in sixty days your life will change dramatically. That's a sure way to set yourself up for disappointment. Yet, life-changing insights can occur from the very beginning."

Nancy is grateful for all the breakthrough moments she's experienced while working with her mentors over the years. She's also equally thankful to be in a position where she is able to help others achieve their own memorable mentorship moments.

Nancy gets involved in her company's summer internship program for college students majoring in business information systems. It's a terrific program that enables students to receive hands-on learning about what it's like to work in the tech industry. One young woman who participated in the internship program for the past two summers sought Nancy's advice concerning a recurring theme in her life. Specifically, when the woman would have a group assignment at school, she regularly found that she ended up contributing the most to get the project completed while the rest of the group contributed very little. The group received a good grade on the project, but she was left feeling unfulfilled by having to carry the load. The intern was concerned that the same scenario would play out again and again after she graduated from college and secured full-time employment.

Nancy's first piece of advice to the young woman was to slow down. One of Nancy's favorite new slogans is "not so fast," because she, herself, tends to jump right in to quickly take care of most situations that present themselves to her. But Nancy has learned there is great value in putting yourself on pause for a moment before jumping into action. Doing so gives you time to gain clarity about what is really needed and how best to take that next step. Nancy helped her intern to see the value in being "not so fast" while still getting the job done under a deadline. She also helped the woman understand that when working in a group, it's common for members of a group is to sit back and let someone else take the initiative and, more often than not, the bulk of the workload. Being "not so fast" helps in this regard as well.

Another piece of advice Nancy gave was to speak up. "I told her if she'd spoken up at the beginning of the project, what she experienced might not have happened. To which my intern replied, 'But I didn't want to make anybody upset, because they had a lot of stuff going on.' I reminded her that they all had an equal commitment to be contributing members of the group and that what she was really doing was people pleasing."

> **❝ I've learned to soften my approach by taking a deep breath before I respond to help take the emotion out of my feedback."**

Nancy made a point to work with the intern on projects throughout the summer so she could have more positive group experiences and practice speaking up to create better outcomes at work and school. And she helped the young women learn how to speak up without damaging relationships—a skill that Nancy continues to develop.

"I never struggled with speaking up, I'm good at that," laughs Nancy. "But I struggle at times with having my words be kind and considerate, because my natural tendency is to call people out. If someone isn't doing their fair share, I'll say 'I'm not doing that by myself. Where are you in all this? You have a commitment. You have to do your part.' I've learned to soften my approach by taking a deep breath before I respond to help take the emotion out of my feedback."

Another strategy Nancy offers to help more effectively deal with people-pleasing tendencies is to learn how to tell others what you would like them to do for you. To illustrate, Nancy shares a story from her personal life.

"My twenty-one-year-old son is my 'roommate,' and I'm grateful our personalities do well together," says Nancy. "Life at home is very peaceful for us. My son doesn't have any major responsibilities around the house, so I started asking him to notice when something needed to be done and to take the initiative to do it. I'm talking about simple things here, like bringing in the trash cans or putting his dirty dishes into the dishwasher rather than leaving them on the counter. Because I don't like to nag, I caught myself being a people pleaser—I just took care of the task myself if he didn't get to it. But that was leaving me feeling resentful and then feeling silly for feeling resentful, and then the negative thoughts would build up, and I would chew him out and disrupt the peace."

What Nancy learned, which she also applies to her work life, is that it helps to give people a simple, short request to do something specific and within a specified timeframe, and then to step back, get out of the way, and let them handle it. "I remember a time when the trash cans were left by the street for a week, and it killed me every day I drove up and they were still there. After the garbage collectors came a week later and the cans were still on the curb, I simply and unemotionally asked my son 'Hey, would you mind putting those trash cans away for me this morning?' and he said 'Okay, Mom'. And it was done."

Nancy believes that the lesson for women is that while it may seem easier to people please and do everything yourself, it actually makes things harder for you. Plus, the other person loses because they miss out on feeling the satisfaction of contributing and being a part of a team. Whether folks admit it or not, when everyone is contributing, it does make a positive difference for all.

> ❝ **When we skip our homework, and many women do, we find ourselves repeatedly in situations that are inequitable—like not receiving equal pay for equal work or taking a job that can set us up for failure."**

Breaking things down for people while being simple and direct also works well in negotiating, another skill Nancy has found to be pivotal in her career as a woman in tech. Because negotiation has been and continues to be a big part of Nancy's job, she's been able to develop her negotiation talents into a real signature strength.

"When it comes to doing well in any negotiation, you have to do your homework," she asserts. "When we skip our homework, and many women do, we find ourselves repeatedly in situations that are inequitable—like not receiving equal pay for equal work or taking a job that can set us up for failure."

Nancy recalls a Harvard Business Review study about minority CEOs—women and people from non-Caucasian races. The study found that many minorities who achieved the status of CEO were offered the top job with the caveat of turning a company around. The organizations they were asked to lead were completely broke, underfunded, or in serious crisis mode. While many of the CEOs studied were able to fix their companies and "save the day," an even larger number were unable to transform the companies because they were too far gone to begin with. The minority CEOs were held accountable for those failures, many of which were well publicized, even though the troubled companies had been struggling long before the new minority CEO stepped into the role.

The study struck a chord with Nancy. "No matter how great an opportunity may sound or how stellar the executive team may be, do your homework on the company, ask the tough questions to understand their equity position and structure, and always negotiate for yourself," she says.

> **While a man can get away with 'I' language, a woman who uses it is still seen as being overly ambitious or a troublemaker."**

Nancy was offered a tempting executive position working with a CEO she adored who has great vision. She didn't jump at the opportunity though. She took her time, met with several of the company's staff and management team members, and participated in an organization-wide meeting to see how the different departments interacted with one another. When it came time to negotiate for her employment package, the company didn't have the funding to pay her what the position in the industry commanded (she did her research on that as well) and for what they were expecting her to accomplish. Through her negotiation abilities, the company said they would meet her salary requirements. However, the offer was contingent on the company getting funding which they had been unable to secure for some time. In the end, Nancy declined the position and felt confident in doing so because she'd done her homework and weighed all the variables. She knew she made a smart decision.

"The other key to negotiating effectively is to know what you want and deserve and then ask for it nicely," says Nancy. "Pay attention to effective women leaders, including high-profile leaders like Hillary Clinton and Sheryl Sandberg. You'll see they use the word 'we' more than they use the word 'I.' 'We' positioning is more effective for women because it sounds less selfish and self-centered. While a man can get away with 'I' language, a woman who uses it is still seen as being overly ambitious or a troublemaker."

While Nancy recognizes there is a double standard when it comes to how men and women negotiate for their own success, she offers several effective and gender-neutral tips. "I've studied body language in negotiations. When you have a point to make or you want to let someone speaking know that you find what they're saying to be important to you, look them straight in the face. At the same time, if you want to take the power position, you can look away to show you're considering what they're saying. You can also look away or at your phone to let them know that they don't have your attention anymore, and you're not interested or aligned with their negotiation point."

Nancy understands that negotiation is not only important in business, but it's a fact of life, and sometimes negotiations can be painful when it comes to personal issues such as going through a divorce, having to take care of an ill family member, or separating from a job. "Whatever life brings to you, stay focused on what's positive in your life, and be grateful for all the people who step up for you in so many meaningful ways each day. You can lament over one person or situation that isn't the way you want it, or you can see that experience in the context of your whole life and all the other wonderful relationships you have."

> **As women, we need to find what works for us, whatever that may be. When you're grounded, you give yourself the greatest chance to be your best and focus on what really matters to you."**

You also have to find a way to be grounded in your life. Nancy centers and grounds herself through breathing, prayer, and meditation every day for an hour upon waking. No matter what's happening in her life, it helps her release any negative energy and connect to what's important. One of her all-time favorite movies is *Broadcast News* with Holly Hunter. In it, Hunter plays an ambitious producer at a network news division in Washington DC. "She's a super smart fireball," says Nancy. "She's strong for all the people she works with, mostly men, and is calm under fire. Yet before she starts her workday and tackles all the craziness, she has a good cry. She really lets it all out! I related to that because it's her way of getting grounded. As women, we need to find what works for us, whatever that may be. When you're grounded, you give yourself the greatest chance to be your best and focus on what really matters to you."

And when you focus on what really matters, a world of beautiful possibilities opens up and becomes available to you, changing your life for the better, and the lives of others as well.

More about Nancy Ridge

Nancy Ridge possesses more than twenty years' experience as a consultant and hands-on executive, including leading a start-up telecommunications reseller (an "Inc. 500" winner). She currently serves as executive vice president at Telecom Brokers (telecombrokers.com) and co-founder and past president of Alliance of Channel Women (allianceofchannelwomen.org), formerly known as Women in the Channel.

Since 2005, Nancy has built national technology consultant and distributor Telecom Brokers into one of the most profitable, high-profile, and successful master agencies in the telecommunications channel. The partner program she created is focused on helping partners take a strategic approach to grow their businesses. Nancy collaborates with Telecom Brokers' more than 150 service providers for bandwidth, voice and cloud/managed services, and more than 350 partners to offer the best solutions and business outcomes to clients while remaining committed to remarkable customer service. Her clients benefit from her extensive experience in business plan modeling, breakthrough sales strategies, ongoing education, and competitive commissions in a personalized, innovation-driven, committed partner ecosystem.

Previously, Nancy was vice president of sales for ATI, where she created and managed the company's indirect sales channel that resulted in achieving over 2,000 percent growth and the #5 slot on the "Inc. 500 Fastest Growing

Companies" list. In the mid- to late-nineties she was vice president for a consulting firm where she pioneered the Telecom Expense Management concept and built a highly successful organization from the ground up. She was also a principal in a demand-side energy service company for ten years.

Nancy is a co-founder and past president of the Alliance of Channel Women, a nonprofit where women in leadership collaborate with other women leaders in the telecommunications and IT industry to grow their businesses, develop personally and professionally, and pass on their experience through mentoring (allianceofchannelwomen. org). The organization was established in 2010.

Over the years, Nancy has built a reputation for her professional skills and specialties such as: collaborating for successful outcomes; building distribution chains; project management; applying cloud computing technology solutions including: security, UCaaS, IaaS, SaaS, Big Data-Analytics, VDI, BDR, MDM, blockchain, SD-WAN, MPLS and IP-VPN networks; internet access—all types; telecom expense management; SIP trunks; local and long distance voice; and wholesale voice and data.

Follow Nancy on LinkedIn (Nancy Ridge) and Twitter (nancy_ridge). She can also be contacted at nancy@ telecombrokers.com.

If you enjoyed the stories in this section, please consider posting a review on Amazon.com. Reviews help readers like you choose books and authors get more readers.

SECTION

II

CHAPTER 18 _____
Your Emotional Needs Matter
_____

Are you ready for the second part of this book?

First, I want you to take a quick moment to reflect on what stood out most for you from the first part of the book. What were some of your key takeaways? Perhaps you want to put some ideas into action. Maybe you had a sense of viewing something differently in your life. Take a moment now to write down your thoughts about what you read in the first part of this book.

Notes:

_____
_____
_____
_____

The first section of the book is rich with insights and advice, to be sure. Personally, I was struck by the extraordinary degree of self-awareness that the women in these chapters possess.

Even more extraordinary than having that self-awareness was that each of these women acted upon their self-knowledge to noticeably improve at least one pivotal aspect of her life.

I think this is remarkable.

And most meaningful.

Meaningful because it further validates the notion that self-awareness, a crucial building block for emotional intelligence, is a predominant factor for success at work and in life.

Here's why I believe this to be true: Having spent a large part of my professional—and who's kidding who, personal waking hours—pondering, researching, teaching, and applying emotional intelligence-building techniques, I have found that self-awareness is the cornerstone of emotional intelligence.

Let me repeat that. **Self-awareness is the cornerstone of emotional intelligence.** If we were building a skyscraper (which is an apt analogy for emotional intelligence), we wouldn't start at the top!

And the cornerstone of self-awareness, in my opinion, is understanding and working with your own emotions.

And the cornerstone of working with your own emotions is understanding and doing something about your emotional needs.

Emotional needs. We will now explore this topic in the second section of this book.

Your emotional needs matter.

When you read those two words—emotional needs—did you feel a reaction to them? What type of reaction was it?

It's important that you check in with yourself when you hear the words "emotional needs," because many of us were taught or conditioned by well-intentioned (and sometimes not-so-well-intentioned) people that having emotional needs is bad. Very bad. Some of us may have been taught that being emotional or having emotional needs is not a sign of strength, but a sign of weakness.

I call B.S. on that, my friends, and I encourage you to do the same. That particular belief, that emotions equal weakness, will keep you from excelling at work, enjoying life, and evolving as a soul.

Emotions are meant to be experienced by human beings. That's the point of our existence to a large, and I mean very large, degree. Emotions are the centerpiece of life.

So, here's what we're going to work on together in this second part of the book. First, I want to talk to you about emotional intelligence in a more general sense, so you understand the big picture thinking behind it and begin to see how self-awareness and, specifically, your emotional needs fit into the framework of emotional intelligence (chapter 19).

And then it's going to get personal. I want to help you attain the insights you need to become even more self-aware, further boosting your emotional intelligence so you can focus on what matters most in your life! To help accomplish this, I have created for you a self-assessment called *Your Top Emotional Needs* (chapter 20), where you will examine forty-four emotional needs. What's really cool about this self-assessment is that you can use it over and over again whenever you feel that things in your life are out of kilter or stuck, or you just need a positive energy boost, or you feel that everything is going as planned—and you want to keep it that way.

Then in the last chapters of this section (chapters 21 and 22), I will guide you through an exercise called *Your Three Stars* to activate your self-awareness of your top emotional needs so that you can take purposeful and inspired action to get those needs met in a way that feels good to you. **When you take positive action to fulfill your top emotional needs, you create space in your life to attract new experiences more in alignment with your purpose and heart's desires.**

Together, the chapters in this section are exceedingly powerful. The knowledge and insights shared, along with the actions you'll take, will help you breathe new energy into your life so you can be the woman in technology you've always imagined while focusing on what matters most to you.

CHAPTER 19

The Big Deal about Emotional Intelligence

Each of us has more intelligence than we are trained to use and the part that we get graded on in school doesn't amount to much.

—Dr. Laurie Nadel, psychotherapist, author of *Sixth Sense: Unlocking Your Ultimate Mind Power*

I'm ecstatic that emotional intelligence is getting some well-deserved attention around the world. It's a frequent topic at the family breakfast table and in corporate boardrooms and, quite frankly, in most scenarios where people interact with people, though they may not necessarily refer to it as Emotional Intelligence.

So, how did this notion of emotional intelligence come to be and what is it?

In the mid-1980s the work of psychologist and Harvard professor, Howard Gardner, forever changed our thinking on intelligence. Gardner is described as being one of the "top one hundred greatest thinkers of our time" and has authored more than twenty books on multiple intelligences. He helped us understand how people learn differently and that **humans do not possess one type of intelligence but can actually possess, to one degree or another, up to nine different types of intelligences.**

Included on Gardner's list of multiple intelligences are: interpersonal; intrapersonal; verbal/linguistic; logical/

mathematical; bodily/kinesthetic; music/rhythmic; visual/spatial; naturalist (how sensitive you are toward nature and the world around you); and existential (your ability to use collective values and intuition to understand people and the world).

But perhaps Dr. Gardner's greatest contribution to humanity is that he helped shine light on why some "smart" people, people with high IQs (those with high verbal/linguistic intelligence and/or logical/mathematical intelligence) fail miserably at work and in life. He found they simply did not possess a high enough level of interpersonal intelligence and/or intrapersonal intelligence. Together, interpersonal and intrapersonal intelligences make up emotional intelligence.

Others who have contributed greatly to the study of emotional intelligence include early pioneers Peter Salovey and John Mayer, as well as Daniel Goleman (who delineated five components of emotional intelligence), and Travis Bradberry and Jean Greaves, authors of the popular book *Emotional Intelligence 2.0* and co-founders of TalentSmart. This book popularized the measure of emotional intelligence, which is called the "Emotional Quotient" or "EQ." (Bradberry is very active on LinkedIn. Follow him!) If you're interested in exploring the topic further, I highly recommend the teachings of all these individuals, whose collective body of work has helped us better understand and appreciate the many facets of emotional intelligence.

Now back to defining emotional intelligence. A widely accepted and one of the more straightforward definitions of

EI is your ability to recognize and understand emotions in yourself and others, and it is your ability to use this awareness to manage your behavior and relationships.

Sounds simple enough, right?

On the contrary, emotional intelligence is among the most complex and difficult topics to appropriately address, because its development opportunities are everywhere and the possibilities for how emotional intelligence can be demonstrated are limitless. And the stakes, especially if you are a businesswoman, are high.

According to the Center for Creative Leadership, researchers estimate that success at work is 80-90 percent EQ (interpersonal and intrapersonal intelligences), and only 10-20 percent IQ (verbal/linguistic and logical/mathematical intelligences). What this means is that being "bright" is simply not enough. And it's certainly not enough for most businesses today, which are becoming increasingly sophisticated and complex. Having a team of people with high IQs alone just doesn't cut it.

Yet, there is hope for all of us, no matter how high or low our emotional intelligence!

Out of all the intelligences, the only ones you can expand beyond what you are born with are the two that make up your emotional intelligence—interpersonal and intrapersonal intelligences. That's not the case with IQ. If your IQ is 96, it's not going to get higher no matter how hard you try. You can still optimize what you do have, but there are limits. Contrast that to your emotional intelligence or the measure of your emotional intelligence, your EQ. **You can keep getting emotionally "smarter" every day, if that's your desire! There is no limit to how much you can expand your emotional intelligence.**

Plus, the more you develop your emotional intelligence, you will strengthen all these other crucial skills that make life easier and more enjoyable: accountability, change openness, customer service, communication, confidence, decision making, empathy, flexibility, social grace, stress reduction, teamwork, time management, and trust.

But there are even more perks. If you are someone who frequently develops and uses her emotional intelligence in a positive way day in and day out, you can pat yourself on the back for experiencing these well-researched and validated benefits: your physical health improves because you respond better to stress; your mental health and wellbeing improve because you have a happier outlook and more positive attitude; your relationships with your colleagues and others become stronger and more fulfilling; and conflicts become easier to perceive, produce less stress, and are easier to resolve.

The truth of the matter is this: when you use your emotional intelligence in a positive way, it puts you in the drivers' seat so you achieve the best possible outcomes, most consistently, at work, and in life!

The Quest for "Positive" Emotional Intelligence

You'll notice that I frequently add the word "positive" in front of "emotional intelligence." You would think the extra word wouldn't be needed because if someone has emotional intelligence that's positive in and of itself, right? Well…not exactly.

Sadly, there are plenty of people who possess what I call "negative" emotional intelligence. While they have the ability to recognize and understand emotions in themselves and others, and the ability to use this awareness to manage their behavior and relationships, *unfortunately* they use their abilities for more nefarious gains. Some of the best cons in the world have high emotional intelligence, especially intrapersonal intelligence. This is how they so effectively lie, swindle, and cheat. They are among the most dangerous of humans.

As such, I'll make the distinction of positive emotional intelligence from time to time.

Emotional Intelligence Assessments and the Assessment You are About to Take

Let me first come right out and tell you I have a bias when it comes to emotional intelligence assessments. And from that bias I've created a different type of assessment that provides a unique starting point for developing your emotional intelligence. It's not better than other assessments, it's just different.[1]

There are numerous outstanding instruments for assessing EQ or EI. Perhaps you have already taken one and found great value. I know I have. I have taken several of these assessments and have a great respect for those who developed them. For me, the challenge with some emotional intelligence assessments is that they can easily create a false positive result because they rely on the person taking the assessment to honestly respond to questions where the "correct" response can be figured out, even though it's not a true response for the test taker. In these cases, the test taker gets the feedback they want to receive, but not the feedback they need.

Add to that the observation that usually the people who really need to develop emotional intelligence (and we all do to some degree or another), don't see that they need to develop it because they don't have the emotional self-awareness to do so! Talk about a catch-22. This is why I'm a firm believer that to develop your emotional intelligence you start with boosting your self-awareness.

Lastly, another challenge I have found in working with emotional intelligence assessments is no matter how you position the assessment, there is a competitive element that cannot be ignored—people want to score high (or low, depending on the assessment). They don't want any perceived weakness to be exposed, they don't want to be seen as "less than," and they are really concerned about sharing their results with others, especially their own managers. The only ones who don't feel this way are the ones who are already exceptionally emotionally intelligent!

I believe we all have the capacity to be incredibly emotionally intelligent no matter where our starting point is. It's not a competition, it's a personal and lifelong journey in which you can excel if that is your desire. A standardized assessment that focuses (even unknowingly) on competition or does not allow for individuality just never made sense to me. I share this with you because, while I recommend taking emotional intelligence assessments, I do have some rather unorthodox approaches to increasing your emotional intelligence, starting with my assessment—the *Your Top Emotional Needs* assessment (chapter 20) and an exercise to activate your insights gained from the assessment called *Your Three Stars* (chapters 21 and 22).

When you take the assessment in the next chapter, you are not taking it to get an overall score that is compared against others. You are taking the assessment to uncover information about what's important to you and only you. You're receiving information on your own emotional needs. This is vital information that matters to you. You will then get a chance to ponder your emotional needs further and take simple actions to get those needs met when you work through the *Your Three Stars* exercise.

Together, the assessment and exercise can lead you to make a seismic shift in how you process your thoughts and emotions. Your work in these last chapters can change the trajectory of your life.

I have found that when you have clarity around your emotional needs and get your most pressing needs met, you are in an excellent position to enhance your self-awareness, which in turn helps you unlock your true potential, move forward in a way that makes the best sense for you, and create a framework for living "easy" and feeling a sense of freedom like you've never felt before!

Oh, and the biproduct of this work is that your overall emotional intelligence will go up.

Now, on to the assessment!

[1] A Bit About My Background

My interest in emotional intelligence began in graduate school when I did my master's of science degree project on Emotional Intelligence and how the purposeful development of it in the workplace significantly contributes to the health and prosperity of organizations and the people in those organizations. Then, in the late 1990s I received my first company-sponsored coaching certification. (I currently hold four certifications, each of which are focused on applying widely accepted emotional intelligence boosting principles and practices.) In the 2000s I was hired by a college in the Chicagoland area to create and facilitate courses to develop emotional intelligence in both adults and youth. In the 2010s I had the good fortune to be hired by a healthcare CEO to head up her organizational development effort to strengthen further staff efficiency, effectiveness, and engagement through signature strengths and, you guessed it, emotional intelligence leadership training.

I knew I was on to something with the mix of training and development programs we implemented. Within eighteen months of rolling out the strengths and emotional intelligence development initiative, the healthcare company was awarded a Best Places to Work in Illinois designation. The award was based on an independent study of best practices and employee satisfaction. Numerous employees wrote additional comments on their survey to commend the company for the personal and professional development training they received, indicating it was a primary factor for giving their employer a high rating. The company CEO was ahead of her time, and I was quite fortunate to have crossed paths with her. I enjoyed eleven years contributing to the healthcare organization she led.

Today, I continue to develop my understanding and application of emotional intelligence-building insights and techniques. I enjoy infusing my emotional intelligence training content into existing training programs for companies across several industries, as well as bringing emotional intelligence leadership workshops to courageous organizations ready for this next level of leader development.

CHAPTER 20 _____

Your Top Emotional Needs **Assessment**

_____

We all have emotional needs. It's what makes us human. Emotional needs are natural and good. Knowing about your personal top emotional needs is even better!

When you can name, understand, and describe your top emotional needs, it's like being able to speak a foreign language fluently and with great comfort and confidence. **When you can speak the language of your own emotions, you're in a better position to use that information to take purposeful action that's in alignment with your greatest desires.**

But there's another benefit as well when you work with your top emotional needs—doing so can have a direct and positive impact on your self-awareness and emotional intelligence. **When you work on your top emotional needs, you raise your emotional intelligence!**

But first you have to identify your top emotional needs.

Here we go.

NOTE: The assessment you are about to take is designed to assist you in identifying your top emotional needs. The results from this assessment are your results. It's one of the reasons you are receiving it in a paper-based format. Unlike certain online assessments, no one will have access to your results but you! If you choose to share your results with others that is your choice.

Please read these instructions before starting your assessment.

Instructions

There are forty-four emotional needs listed. For each emotional need, start by reading the description of the need presented, then ask yourself the question "How important is this need to me?" Without much thought (go with your gut response), circle the number on the continuum that best represents your response. Then move on to the next need listed.

Do your best to take the entire assessment in a quiet area without interruption. Allot roughly twenty to twenty-five minutes to complete the assessment, though you can take as long as you like. **Remember any answer you have is the right answer for you, so go with the first response that comes to you, which is typically the truest.**

I hope you enjoy the assessment!

Emotional Need #1

To feel accepted

It's important that me and my ideas are approved without judgment.

How important is this need to me?

1	2	3	4	5	6	7	8	9	10

Not Important   Somewhat Important   Very Important

Emotional Need #2

To feel acknowledged

It's important that I am recognized with a greeting or glance.

How important is this need to me?

1	2	3	4	5	6	7	8	9	10

Not Important   Somewhat Important   Very Important

Emotional Need #3

To feel admired

It's important that I am warmly or favorably regarded.

How important is this need to me?

1	2	3	4	5	6	7	8	9	10

Not Important   Somewhat Important   Very Important

Emotional Need #4
To feel appreciated
It's important that I am recognized and my worth is valued.

How important is this need to me?

1	2	3	4	5	6	7	8	9	10

Not Important   **Somewhat**   **Very Important**
                                  Important

Emotional Need #5
To feel approved of
It's important that who I am or what I do is good or acceptable.

How important is this need to me?

1	2	3	4	5	6	7	8	9	10

Not Important   **Somewhat**   **Very Important**
                                  Important

Emotional Need #6
To feel believed in
It's important that I have confidence in what I do and say.

How important is this need to me?

1	2	3	4	5	6	7	8	9	10

Not Important   **Somewhat**   **Very Important**
                                  Important

Emotional Need #7
To feel a calling
It's important that I have a mission or a purpose in my life.

How important is this need to me?

1	2	3	4	5	6	7	8	9	10

Not Important   **Somewhat**   **Very Important**
                           Important

Emotional Need #8
To feel capable
It's important that I have the ability, fitness, or quality necessary to do or achieve a specified thing.

How important is this need to me?

1	2	3	4	5	6	7	8	9	10

Not Important   **Somewhat**   **Very Important**
                           Important

Emotional Need #9
To feel challenged
It's important that I do things that test my abilities or stretch my capabilities.

How important is this need to me?

1	2	3	4	5	6	7	8	9	10

Not Important   **Somewhat**   **Very Important**
                           Important

Emotional Need #10
To feel clarity (not confused)
It's important that I have a complete understanding of what is being communicated to me.

How important is this need to me?

1	2	3	4	5	6	7	8	9	10

Not Important   **Somewhat Important**   **Very Important**

Emotional Need #11
To feel competent
It's important that I have the necessary ability, knowledge, or skill to do something successfully.

How important is this need to me?

1	2	3	4	5	6	7	8	9	10

Not Important   **Somewhat Important**   **Very Important**

Emotional Need #12
To feel confident
It's important that I have certainty in myself and self-assurance.

How important is this need to me?

1	2	3	4	5	6	7	8	9	10

Not Important   **Somewhat Important**   **Very Important**

Emotional Need #13

To feel connected

It's important that I join or link with others for access and/or communications.

How important is this need to me?

1	2	3	4	5	6	7	8	9	10

Not Important   **Somewhat**   **Very Important**
                                  Important

Emotional Need #14

To feel forgiven

It's important that I stop feeling angry or resentful for an offense, flaw, or mistake I have made.

How important is this need to me?

1	2	3	4	5	6	7	8	9	10

Not Important   **Somewhat**   **Very Important**
                                  Important

Emotional Need #15

To feel forgiving

It's important that I stop feeling angry or resentful toward an offense, flaw, or mistake made by another.

How important is this need to me?

1	2	3	4	5	6	7	8	9	10

Not Important   **Somewhat**   **Very Important**
                                  Important

Emotional Need #16
To feel free
It's important that I am not under the control or in the power of another and to act or do as I wish.

How important is this need to me?

1	2	3	4	5	6	7	8	9	10

Not Important   **Somewhat Important**   **Very Important**

Emotional Need #17
To feel friendship
It's important that I have close associations or bonds with others.

How important is this need to me?

1	2	3	4	5	6	7	8	9	10

Not Important   **Somewhat Important**   **Very Important**

Emotional Need #18
To feel fulfilled
It's important that I am satisfied or happy because I've developed my abilities or character.

How important is this need to me?

1	2	3	4	5	6	7	8	9	10

Not Important   **Somewhat Important**   **Very Important**

Emotional Need #19
To feel harmonious
It's important that I am free from disagreement or dissent.

How important is this need to me?

1	2	3	4	5	6	7	8	9	10

Not Important   **Somewhat**   **Very Important**
                            Important

Emotional Need #20
To feel heard
It's important that I am listened or paid attention to.

How important is this need to me?

1	2	3	4	5	6	7	8	9	10

Not Important   **Somewhat**   **Very Important**
                            Important

Emotional Need #21
To feel helped
It's important that others make it easier for me to do something by offering their services or resources.

How important is this need to me?

1	2	3	4	5	6	7	8	9	10

Not Important   **Somewhat**   **Very Important**
                            Important

Emotional Need #22

To feel helpful

It's important that I provide assistance or give help.

How important is this need to me?

1	2	3	4	5	6	7	8	9	10

Not Important   **Somewhat**   **Very Important**
                    Important

Emotional Need #23

To feel important

It's important that I have great significance, value, rank, or status.

How important is this need to me?

1	2	3	4	5	6	7	8	9	10

Not Important   **Somewhat**   **Very Important**
                    Important

Emotional Need #24

To feel in control

It's important that I am able to direct a situation, person, or activity.

How important is this need to me?

1	2	3	4	5	6	7	8	9	10

Not Important   **Somewhat**   **Very Important**
                    Important

Emotional Need #25

To feel included

It's important that I'm allowed to share in an activity or privilege.

How important is this need to me?

1	2	3	4	5	6	7	8	9	10

Not Important   **Somewhat**   **Very Important**
                          Important

Emotional Need #26

To feel listened to

It's important that what I say, including my advice and/or requests, is acted upon.

How important is this need to me?

1	2	3	4	5	6	7	8	9	10

Not Important   **Somewhat**   **Very Important**
                          Important

Emotional Need #27

To feel loved

It's important that I am cared for deeply.

How important is this need to me?

1	2	3	4	5	6	7	8	9	10

Not Important   **Somewhat**   **Very Important**
                          Important

Emotional Need #28
To feel needed
It's important that my assistance or something I have is required because it's essential or very important.

How important is this need to me?

| 1 | 2 | 3 | 4 | 5 | 6 | 7 | 8 | 9 | 10 |

Not Important   **Somewhat Important**   **Very Important**

Emotional Need #29
To feel noticed
It's important that I am given some degree of attention or recognition.

How important is this need to me?

| 1 | 2 | 3 | 4 | 5 | 6 | 7 | 8 | 9 | 10 |

Not Important   **Somewhat Important**   **Very Important**

Emotional Need #30
To feel orderly
It's important that my environment is neat and methodically arranged.

How important is this need to me?

| 1 | 2 | 3 | 4 | 5 | 6 | 7 | 8 | 9 | 10 |

Not Important   **Somewhat Important**   **Very Important**

Emotional Need #31
To feel passion
It's important that I have an intense desire or enthusiasm for something.

How important is this need to me?

1	2	3	4	5	6	7	8	9	10

Not Important   Somewhat   Very Important
                       Important

Emotional Need #32
To feel peaceful
It's important that I am tranquil and free from disturbance.

How important is this need to me?

1	2	3	4	5	6	7	8	9	10

Not Important   Somewhat   Very Important
                       Important

Emotional Need #33
To feel private
It's important that my thoughts/feelings are not shared.

How important is this need to me?

1	2	3	4	5	6	7	8	9	10

Not Important   Somewhat   Very Important
                       Important

Emotional Need #34
To feel productive
It's important that I achieve or produce a significant amount or result.

How important is this need to me?

1	2	3	4	5	6	7	8	9	10

Not Important   **Somewhat**   **Very Important**
                                     Important

Emotional Need #35
To feel reassured
It's important that any doubts I may have are dispelled.

How important is this need to me?

1	2	3	4	5	6	7	8	9	10

Not Important   **Somewhat**   **Very Important**
                                     Important

Emotional Need #36
To feel recognized
It's important that who I am and/or what I do is identified, acknowledged, or appreciated.

How important is this need to me?

1	2	3	4	5	6	7	8	9	10

Not Important   **Somewhat**   **Very Important**
                                     Important

Emotional Need #37
To feel respected
It's important that my abilities, qualities, or achievements are admired or held in high regard.

How important is this need to me?

1	2	3	4	5	6	7	8	9	10

Not Important   **Somewhat Important**   **Very Important**

Emotional Need #38
To feel safe/secure
It's important that I am protected from or not exposed to danger, harm, or risk.

How important is this need to me?

1	2	3	4	5	6	7	8	9	10

Not Important   **Somewhat Important**   **Very Important**

Emotional Need #39
To feel supported
It's important that I have approval, comfort, or encouragement.

How important is this need to me?

1	2	3	4	5	6	7	8	9	10

Not Important   **Somewhat Important**   **Very Important**

Emotional Need #40
To feel fairly treated
It's important that I am handled with justice or dealt with equitably.

How important is this need to me?

1	2	3	4	5	6	7	8	9	10

Not Important   **Somewhat**   **Very Important**
                           Important

Emotional Need #41
To feel trusted
It's important that my reliability, words, abilities, or strengths are believed in.

How important is this need to me?

1	2	3	4	5	6	7	8	9	10

Not Important   **Somewhat**   **Very Important**
                           Important

Emotional Need #42
To feel understood
It's important that my explanations or words are comprehended or perceived as intended.

How important is this need to me?

1	2	3	4	5	6	7	8	9	10

Not Important   **Somewhat**   **Very Important**
                           Important

Emotional Need #43
To feel valued
It's important that I am considered to be important or beneficial.

How important is this need to me?

1	2	3	4	5	6	7	8	9	10

Not Important   **Somewhat**   **Very Important**
Important

Emotional Need #44
To feel worthy
It's important that I have or show qualities or abilities that merit recognition and/or respect.

How important is this need to me?

1	2	3	4	5	6	7	8	9	10

Not Important   **Somewhat**   **Very Important**
Important

CHAPTER 21 _____

Your Three Stars **Exercise**

_____

Let's Now Get to Work on Your Needs

Whew! You made it through the process of examining all forty-four emotional needs listed on the assessment. Now what?

In this chapter you will find meaning from your responses as you 1) determine which emotional needs matter most to you right now; 2) create some simple strategies to get your top needs met; 3) choose an action step you will commit to for one of your top needs, and 4) take that action.

The process can be miraculous.

When you take inspired action to get one of your emotional needs met, it actually helps to meet other needs as well. **With every need met, you need less. When you need less, you worry less and have more space in your life to focus on what matters most. And when your emotional wellbeing improves, it has a direct and positive impact on your self-awareness and emotional intelligence.** This is one incredibly powerful way to raise your EQ!

Having certain or too many unmet needs drains your energy in a way that makes it difficult to be your best emotionally and do your best work. And it also makes it very hard to raise your emotional intelligence. This will make more sense to you once you start working with *Your Three Stars* and get at least one of your unmet needs met. You will be amazed at how good you will feel.

Note: Take the time you need to complete this exercise. I recommend that you give yourself permission to start the exercise, think about it overnight, let your insights bubble up for you organically, and then finish the exercise.

This exercise is actually a process that once learned, you can revisit time and time again whenever you feel anxious, confused, or stuck—or feel absolutely wonderful and want to keep it that way!

We'll now work through the six steps of the exercise over the next several pages.

Step #1

Your first step is to determine which three of the forty-four needs are most pressing in your life right now. Recognize they will most assuredly change over time, and as you get one need met, another need might bubble up to the top for you. For this exercise, really focus on those needs that you think about most.

Go back to chapter 19 and take a look at the needs you rated the highest or as being the most important to you.

For the purpose of this exercise, your goal is to determine which of your top emotional needs would make your list of top three. You don't need to rank them at this time. Just come up with your top three.

It's perfectly fine if you have more than three top needs or have no top needs—maybe you rated your top needs as not being very important. Either way, I'd like you to look at your results and determine which three of your needs are most important to you right now. These will be the three that we will use to work on *Your Three Stars* exercise together.

When you have your top three emotional needs identified, you're ready for Step 2.

Step #2

Take a look at the three blank pages that follow. Starting with the first blank page, see the lines above each star? Good. Use the first line to write in one of your top identified needs. Then use the second line to write in the description that relates to that need. (You'll find this on the assessment in the previous chapter. It's the sentence right under the top need you identified and wrote on the first line.)

Repeat this process for each of your three identified needs so that the top section above the star on each of the blank pages is complete.

A top emotional need I have is: _____

_____

This means it's important that: _____

_____

My Action Statement: _____

_____

A top emotional need I have is: _____

_____

This means it's important that: _____

_____

My Action Statement: _____

_____

A top emotional need I have is: _____

_____

This means it's important that: _____

_____

My Action Statement: _____

_____

Step #3

For each of the top three needs you identified, you're going to repeat the activities below.

You will need three blank pieces of paper, one for each star, in order to complete this step. This step includes a series of activities. You can also take notes digitally on an electronic device, though I do recommend writing out your responses.

Activity A

Take a look at <u>one</u> of your top three needs. On a blank piece of paper, just start writing down all the ways you could get that need met. Don't think too long or hard about your list. This activity is really nothing more than a brain dump for that particular emotional need.

- Write down all the things you can do *personally* to get the need met for yourself. Write out "I can…" and then complete the sentence by writing out what you can do to meet your need.

For example, an idea to meet your need "to feel confident" could be something as simple as *"I can run through my presentation tonight with my daughter before my meeting tomorrow"* or *"I can dry-clean my favorite outfit so I can wear it when I meet my new boss next week."*

- Write down all the things that *others could do* for you to take care of your need. Write out "[insert name of person] can..." and then complete the sentence by writing out what that person can do to meet your need.

For example, something that others could do for you to help meet your need "to feel confident" could be *"Mark can make me my favorite coffee drink before I leave for my interview tomorrow"* or *"Ariana can schedule me to meet with Jessica first thing in the morning when my energy is best."*

It doesn't matter if your ideas are simple or complex at this point. Again, just write them all down without editing yourself or judging what you write.

When you've exhausted your list, move on to the next activity.

Activity B

Look at the ideas you listed in Activity A for getting your particular emotional need met.

- Now quickly go through your list of ideas, and circle the ones that you sense/feel/think would be the simplest or easiest for you to put into action.

Again, no need to agonize much. Let your inner guidance assist you. If it feels right to you, just circle it.

- Now, looking at the ideas you circled, which would be your top five ideas? Identify the five ideas you think would be the simplest or easiest to complete to help meet your emotional need.

If you have fewer than five ideas circled, that's okay.

IMPORTANT: Take a close look at the ideas you have listed that describe an action **you** can take to meet your emotional need, rather than having someone else meet that need for you. These ideas have the highest likelihood of producing the result you most desire because you have more control of the outcome. It can be quite difficult for someone else to meet your need exactly the way you want it to be met. For more on this, take a look at chapter 22 in the section titled "Get More of Your Emotional Needs Met…On Your Own."

Activity C

Now, write one of your top five circled ideas on one of the points of the star relating to that particular need. Continue writing your other top five ideas on the other points of the star until all points of the star have an idea written on them. The ideas all describe actions you can take to help get your emotional need met.

Repeat

- Repeat Activity A, B, and C for each of your other top emotional needs you identified in Step 1.

When you have three completed stars, move on to Step 4.

See next page for a sample of a completed star.

Sample

A top emotional need I have is: To feel challenged

This means it's important that: It's important that I do things that test my abilities or stretch my capabilities.

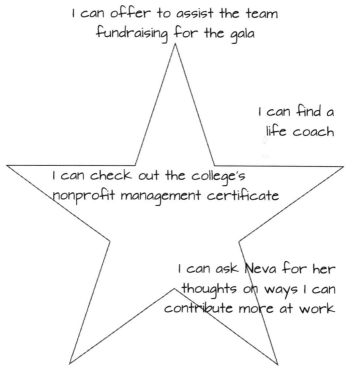

I can offer to assist the team fundraising for the gala

I can find a life coach

I can check out the college's nonprofit management certificate

I can ask Neva for her thoughts on ways I can contribute more at work

I can sign up for that improv comedy class I always wanted to take

Step 4

Now take a look at all three of your completed stars as a whole. Place them side by side so you can view them all at once.

Which of your top three emotional needs seems or feels to you to be your greatest need at this time? This is the need that can consume your thinking on any given day.

- **While focusing on the star relating to your greatest emotional need at this time, look at the ideas you have written on each of the points of the star.** Which of these five ideas can you most easily put into action over the next seventy-two hours? If you have more than one, identify the one that you are most willing to commit to put into action. Highlight this idea in some way—circle it, highlight it in your favorite color, put an asterisk by it, whatever you'd like to do to make it stand out to you.

Now that you have highlighted this particular idea, ask yourself this question: **Will this idea, if put into action, feel good to me with no negative side effects?** If your answer is "yes" then complete the "My Action Statement" section under the star using the words in the box below. If you answered the question "Will this idea if put into action feel good to me with no negative side effects?" with a "no" then go back and select another one of your ideas that feels good with no negative side effects. This will increase your odds of getting your need met.

- **My Action Statement:** I will (write in the action idea you just highlighted). I am putting this into motion now and will either complete this action or a first step toward completing it within the next seventy-two hours.

Ultimately, you want to select an idea you will commit to put into action as soon as possible and, ideally, within the next seventy-two hours. If you can't commit to putting it into action within a week, pick another idea from your star points to put into action that you can more easily accomplish in the time frame.

NOTE: What's important here is that you are taking that first step to put your idea into action and having one of your top emotional needs met. Some ideas may require more time, but once you put it into action and take that initial step, you increase the chance of your success.

To illustrate, here's a sample of how your *My Action Statement* could look. (The emotional need being addressed is the need "to feel helpful.")

I will put together and share with my boss a description of a one-hour training session I would like to create and facilitate on the topic of leveraging distributed ledger/blockchain technologies. I am putting this into motion now and will complete this action within the next seventy-two hours.

Step 5

Take a look at the remaining two stars. Place them together so you can view them both at once.

Which of these two emotional needs seems to be your second greatest need at this time? You don't spend as much time thinking about this need as the need identified in Step 4, but it still is a top need for you.

- **Just as you did in Step 4, look at the ideas you've written on each of the points of the star relating to this second greatest emotional need.** Which one of those ideas listed can you most easily put into action in the next seventy-two-hour period? Highlight the idea in some way—circle it, highlight it in your favorite color, put an asterisk by it, whatever you'd like to do to make it stand out to you.

Finally, in the "My Action Statement" section under the star, write and complete this sentence:

- **My Action Statement:** I will (write in your idea you will commit to put into action). I am putting this into motion now and will complete this action within the next seventy-two hours.

Another sample of a completed *My Action Statement* is (for the emotional need "to feel important"):

I will update my email signature block to include my recent Advanced IofT Certification. I am putting this into motion now and will complete this action within the next seventy-two hours.

Step 6

This is the last step (for now), and it's a bit counterintuitive.

Stay with me.

I want you to put your attention this week on the My Action Statement you wrote for your second-most pressing emotional need. Yes, that's right, the *My Action Statement* you wrote in Step 5.

Why start by taking care of your second-most pressing emotional need?

First of all, there's a good chance it's actually easier for you to tackle your second-most pressing emotional need because there is a lesser, even if it's a slightly lesser, emotional charge attached to that second need. And it's still important to you so you're still motivated to accomplish it.

Plus, with that first success under your belt, you will find it easier to put into motion your *My Action Statement* for your first, or more pressing emotional need, which can be more difficult to tackle. When you accomplish the task of meeting your second emotional need (or at least feeling better about it), you can move on to activating the action statement to help fill your first emotional need. Then, in a relatively short period of time, you'll have two of your top emotional needs either met or well on their way to being met. You will notice a difference in how you respond to what life throws your way, you'll experience more positive results, life will feel easier, and you'll have a greater self-awareness around your emotions in general.

Note: You may very well prefer to tackle your greatest emotional need first. That is perfectly acceptable. I'm sure you will crush it!

Again, everyone is different. **The feedback I've received from clients is that it's often easier for them to take action on their second-most pressing emotional need.** The same may be true for you. Then, once you start to feel that need is met, either your first need is not as pressing and/or is easier for you to fulfill. And you end up feeling better and more fulfilled around two of your top emotional needs in a shorter period of time.

When you get your unmet needs met, that translates into feeling lighter, more optimistic, and freer. You'll be better able to more effectively handle other issues that come up in your workday with greater peacefulness and ease.

Your Remaining Star

What do you do with the ideas you wrote down to fill the needs of your last remaining star?

The more emotional needs you fill the better. After you fill your top two needs, see how you feel about tackling your third top need. Go through Step 4 and Step 5 again to determine and put into action that one idea to get your third emotional need met and then make the commitment to take that action.

Alternatively, you may find that your third need is not as pressing anymore. You may find other needs have popped up on your "top three" list. If that's the case for you, start at Step 1 again, and go through the complete process.

Furthermore, if you found you struggled to fill your top two needs, no problem. Tackle any one of your other identified top needs. The key is to take focused action to fill a need!

And you could choose to do absolutely nothing with your remaining star at this time. Some people feel so much better after going through the exercise and focusing on their second need (and/or first need) that they just need less. They feel satisfied and in the flow of their life.

Remember, *Your Three Stars* **is truly a process you can access over and over again and whenever you'd like over the course of your lifetime.** And you'll know when it's time to engage *Your Three Stars* and get your emotional needs met by how you feel. If you feel your negative emotions piling up, that's a good time to activate one of *Your Three Stars*!

CHAPTER 22 _____
Keep Moving Forward
___

You will find as you get your top emotional needs met, you need less and have a greater capacity to attract people, places, and things into your life that lift you up and energize you. You also put yourself in an outstanding position to gain clarity in your life so you can focus on what matters most. I want to take a moment now to share another simple exercise to help keep your emotional intelligence development moving forward.

For the next couple of months, pay attention to your feelings. When you feel a positive emotion, take the time to name that emotion and recognize what contributed to you having that positive emotion.

Also, when you name your emotion, be specific. Rather than say you feel "good," drill down into that feeling. Do you feel more "fulfilled" or "satisfied" or "euphoric" or "expectant" or "inspired"? Those words tell a different story—to yourself and to others. Again, you want to accurately identify how you are feeling. It makes a stronger connection within yourself, and when you're communicating with others, it helps you more accurately convey your feelings, which can lead to you having more breakthrough and meaningful communications.

On the flipside, when you feel a negative emotion, take the time to name that emotion and recognize what contributed to you feeling that negative emotion. And when you name your negative emotion, be as specific and descriptive as possible.

Rather than say you feel "bad," really dig into your vocabulary bank. Other emotions such as "angry" or "depressed" or "lethargic" or "rejected" or "trapped" are more descriptive. The more descriptive you are, the more you can get under that emotion to examine it and deal with it more effectively. Plus, when you use more descriptive words with others, it can help them better understand how you're feeling and how they could potentially support you.

Look in the Appendix for a list of positive and negative emotions to help you describe your emotions more precisely. As humans we have a wide range of emotions, but many of us only use a small handful of words to describe how we're feeling. When you broaden your emotional vocabulary, you build your emotional self-awareness, which, in turn, further strengthens your emotional intelligence.

Also, when you become more aware of your emotions, you are better able to let your self-awareness guide you to do additional inner work if needed. For example, let's say you find or feel that your days are becoming filled with more negative than positive emotions. This is a cue to take out *Your Three Stars* exercise and get to work. When you identify and fulfill an emotional need that's meaningful to you, you will experience more positive emotions. And you know what happens when you experience more positive emotions, don't you? Your number of fabulous, feel-good days goes up!

Get More of Your Emotional Needs Met...On Your Own

The chances are good that during your lifetime you will experience an emotional need that's important to you that you feel you cannot meet or address through your own actions. You may feel that the only way the need could be met is if someone else, other than you, were to do something for you to meet the need. This is not always feasible or as necessary as you may think.

I'm not saying to *not* ask someone to help you meet one of your emotional needs. You probably know a handful of people who would be more than happy to do that for you. What I'm saying is that it's usually not necessary. You have the capacity to have most your emotional needs met through your own efforts. You also may very well be significantly more satisfied with the results.

For years, I had a strong emotional need "to be heard," especially by my parents. I love them dearly and wanted them to hear what I had to share regarding their health and wellbeing. Both of them have heart disease. My father had a stroke. My mother a heart attack and diabetes diagnosis. Both attributed their illnesses to "old age." I would share information with them to the contrary. I am a longtime advocate and student of the "you are what you eat" school of thinking and hold certifications from the Institute of Integrative Nutrition as a drugless practitioner and health counselor. I thought that if my parents listened to me, that would fix my need to be heard by them (and improve their lives). Well, surprise, surprise—that was not how I got my need to be heard met. I had to get my need met another way.

What did I do? I stopped trying to teach my parents. As the old story goes, you can be the best teacher in the world, but if the student isn't ready to learn, you have nothing to teach her.

Instead, I put myself in a position where I could share my understanding and information with others who were interested in learning about what I had to say. I created a workshop around health and wellbeing for employees at a healthcare organization with which I was working at the time. The employees attracted to the workshop came, participated in it, and loved it. I got my need to be heard met by sharing the information and helping others. I felt so much better and was more loving when I was around my parents from that day forward.

I realized that I was unwittingly projecting much anger toward my parents because they didn't want to hear what I had to share with them on improving their health and wellbeing. Today, they are becoming increasingly open to eating foods that produce more positive results in their lives, and I am thrilled for them.

You see, you *can* get your emotional needs met in some wonderful ways when you focus on what you can do to fulfill an unmet need, rather than relying on someone else to fill it for you.

Last Thoughts

The topic of emotional intelligence is complex and broad. It's one of the most difficult topics to master, because your emotional intelligence has multiple aspects and the ways to develop your emotional intelligence are limitless. And, as of the date this book was published, there is no "top" number on the Emotional Quotient scale—the measure of Emotional Intelligence. In this respect, emotional intelligence as we currently understand it, can be infinite. That means you can keep developing it beyond what you have today or any day in the future, if you have the desire. Wrap your head around that!

The goal of this second section was to introduce you to the concept of Emotional Intelligence and give you a practical tool to help develop your self-awareness—*Your Three Stars. Your Three Stars* is one of many, many ways to develop your self-awareness, and I encourage you to check out the work of the individuals I referenced in chapter 18 or do a web search. If you find a way to develop your emotional intelligence in a positive way that makes sense to you, give it a go. Really, you can't go wrong.

You will find as you work through exercises such as *Your Three Stars* or others designed to help you get your emotional needs met and especially when your needs are met through your own efforts, you become emotionally "lighter" and more self-aware of your emotions. **As you become emotionally lighter, you will have more space in your days, along with more energy so you can do more of the things you truly love to do—those things that matter most to you.** And when you do what matters most to you with no harmful side effects, to yourself and others, that positive energy also raises your emotional intelligence. It's a wonderful, beautiful circle that gives you life. (Cue music from *The Lion King*.)

For those of you who may not have a clear sense of what matters most in your life right now, I recommend working with a coach, taking a self-development workshop, or picking up one of the myriad books on self-development. Let your intuition guide you.

If you haven't read my first book—*How to Be a Woman in Business (while Being True to Yourself)*—consider checking it out. In it is a powerful self-exploration exercise called *Your Seven Circles©* that helps you look within to better understand your strengths, values, and desires. It also shows you how to take inspired action to create a career (and life) that aligns with who you really are—your truth.

Additionally, when you combine insights from *Your Seven Circles* and *Your Three Stars* you can more effectively deal with the world around you, which appears to be getting more complicated by the day! **One sure way to make sense of what's whirling around us is to make sense of what's whirling within.** Both these exercises are designed to help you tap into your own inner knowing to gain clarity and wisdom that matters to you.

So here we are. I hoped you enjoyed this book as much as I enjoyed bringing it to you. I'm excited and honored that we've shared this experience together and look forward to sharing more insights with you in the months to come.

Keep moving forward on your personal journey of self-discovery and innovation. As a woman in technology, this is already in your DNA—you live and breathe it each day through the work you do. **Now is the time to work on you.** It's your time to be a woman in technology who focuses on what matters most.

If you enjoyed this book, please consider posting a review on Amazon.com. Reviews help readers like you choose books and authors get more readers.

APPENDIX

Here is a starter list of positive and negative emotions. Next time you use a word like "happy" or "good" or "sad" or "bad" to describe a feeling you may be having, challenge yourself to expand your emotional vocabulary by using an even more deeply descriptive word. Use this list to help you jumpstart your thinking.

Also, add your own favorite words to this list to more fully and accurately describe your emotions. When you can accurately name your emotions, you enhance your self-awareness, the cornerstone to emotional intelligence.

NOTE: At the end of each day, it's good to check in with yourself to see if you're experiencing fifty-one-percent or more positive emotions. If you have a series of days where you're experiencing more negative emotions than positive, this is a good cue to work on *Your Three Stars* exercise.

Positive Emotions
Accomplished
Able
Agile
Assured
Awesome
(In) Awe
Bright
Brilliant
Capable
Certain

Charmed
Cheerful
Comfortable
Compassionate
Confident
Courageous
Delighted
Determined
Eager
Elated
Empathetic
Encouraged
Energetic
Enthused
Excellent
Expectant
Fantastic
Fascinated
Glad
Glamorous
Gorgeous
Graceful
Grateful
Glorious
Hopeful
Humorous
Influential
Inspired

Interested
Intrigued
Joyful
Jazzed
Loved
Magnanimous
Motivated
Moved
Playful
Peaceful
Pleasant
Pleased
Pleasure
Poised
Positive
Powerful
Remarkable
Relaxed
Relieved
Respected
Satisfied
Stable
Stimulated
Sublime
Superb
Superior
Surprised
Sympathetic

Thrilled

Treasured

Vibrant

Vivacious

Wonderful

Worthy

Negative Emotions

Abandoned

Abused

Aggravated

Alone

Angry

Annoyed

Anxious

Appalled

Awful

Bored

Confused

Deserted

Disappointed

Disgusted

Disoriented

Embarrassed

Envious

Fearful

Frustrated

Guilty

Helpless

Hopeless

Horrible

Indecisive

Indifferent

Inferior

Infuriated

Insecure

Insignificant

Irritated

Irritable

Isolated

Jammed

Jealous

Judged

Jumbled

Livid

Lonely

Misinterpreted

Misread

Misunderstood

Mistreated

Muddled

Neglected

Picked on

Rejected

Self-conscious

Stuck

Terrible
Tired
Trapped
Uncomfortable
Unimportant
Uninterested
Useless
Worthless

ABOUT MISSION SISTERS WHO WORK

All proceeds from this book go to support Mission Sisters Who Work—a humanitarian nonprofit organization co-founded by author Cheryl O'Donoghue and her husband Mark O'Donoghue. The purpose of Mission Sisters Who Work is to provide grants to nonprofit, education, and community organizations serving low-income women working or planning careers in business. The funding provided enables these organizations to offer, at no cost to participants, professional development books and training created by author and human potential advocate, Cheryl O'Donoghue.

With your book purchase, you are now part of a growing movement to provide self-empowerment education to women who experience financial and social barriers, barriers which often prevent them from participating in programs that support their growth and equality in the workplace. You are a true "mission sister," and we are humbled by your support.

The founders at Mission Sisters Who Work believe it is truly an exciting and challenging time for women. But it is not a time for blame or anger. It is a time to be focused and well informed. It is a time to treat each other with respect and dignity. And it is a time to keep the movement moving forward. Please consider sharing the mission with your family and friends who value women's rights in the workplace and in giving women opportunities to be their best selves so that they can serve others with their talents.

Learn more at missionsisterswhowork.org.

MORE ABOUT THE AUTHOR

Cheryl O'Donoghue, MS, is a businesswoman, author, and leadership and human potential advocate. She is president of Emotional Intelligence Leadership Training Solutions, LLC, and co-founder of the humanitarian organization Mission Sisters Who Work (missionsisterswhowork.org). She is also a guest presenter at women's events and organizations, inspiring audiences to act in ways that give their lives more meaning and purpose.

Over the years, Cheryl's writing has appeared in numerous business publications across the financial services, contact center, healthcare, and corporate training industries. Her book *How to Be a Woman in Business (while Being True to Yourself)* was released in February 2018. Cheryl recently completed the book *How to Be a Woman in Technology (while Focusing on What Matters Most)*, and she is in the process of writing a new book on emotional intelligence leadership with a target publishing date in 2020.

Cheryl began her professional career working in computer magnetic storage sales while she paid her way through college. Upon graduation, she landed a job in broadcasting as a radio personality and then transitioned to business marketing and communications. Cheryl also enjoys success designing and facilitating engaging programs that build skills in emotional intelligence leadership, an area in which she has added to her subject matter expertise over the years.

Before starting her own consulting practice and co-founding Mission Sisters Who Work, Cheryl held the position of chief communications officer, vice president of human resources and marketing for VNA Health Care and before that senior vice president for Financial Training Resources; as well as other executive roles in technology-based learning and development, healthcare, and financial services organizations.

Cheryl earned a master of science degree in adult business education from Northern Illinois University, a bachelor of arts double majoring in broadcast communications and marketing from North Central College, Naperville, Illinois, and several industry certifications as an executive and business coach. She served on the faculty at Harper College for several years, designing and teaching personal growth courses for the college's continuing education department and InZone program for youth and continues to serve as a guest lecturer.

Also by **Cheryl O'Donoghue**:
*How to Be a Woman in Business
(while Being True to Yourself)*

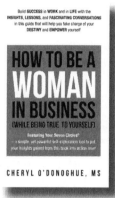

Build **SUCCESS** in **WORK** and in **LIFE** with the
INSIGHTS, LESSONS, and **FASCINATING CONVERSATIONS**
in this guide that will help you take charge of your
DESTINY and **EMPOWER** yourself

HOW TO BE A
WOMAN
IN BUSINESS
(WHILE BEING TRUE TO YOURSELF)

Featuring Your Sense Circles®
— a simple, yet powerful self-exploration tool to put
your insights gained from this book into action now!

CHERYL O'DONOGHUE, MS

"I intended to skim this book to get the gist of it but was
immediately sucked in. Love it!"
—Khali Henderson, Senior Partner
www.buzztheorystrategies.com

"I love Cheryl's engaging writing style and how she
captured important advice and guidance from impressive
and authentic women—including herself!"
—Jacqui Neurauter, BodyMind Therapist and Coach,
president and co-founder of the Veterans Restorative
Project
www.harmoniouspathways.com

How to Be a Woman in Business is a provocative, quick
read for all women—whether you've just started a career in

business or have already logged a few miles and are ready to get re-inspired.

Author Cheryl O'Donoghue, a successful businesswoman and certified business and life coach, interviews seven fascinating women and shares practical insights—lessons learned and real-life stories that will encourage you to become the self-empowered businesswoman you were meant to be.

Learn how to recognize and apply success strategies from relatable women; determine your financial value at work and ask for promotions and salary bumps with confidence; create more productive business relationships; overcome obstacles in the workplace; and develop a heightened sense of self-awareness.

Cheryl also shares a powerful self-exploration exercise she calls *Your Seven Circles©*, which helps you look within to better understand your strengths, values, and desires, and then shows you how to take inspired action to create a career that aligns with who you really are and what's most important to you in life.

Be true to yourself. This book shows you how!

53309938R00183

Made in the USA
Columbia, SC
14 March 2019